The Straight Skinny
Divorce 101

Clarity Through Chaos

Jodi Lynn Silbermann

www.PublishABestSellingBook.com

The Straight Skinny-Divorce 101

Clarity Through Chaos

Jodi Lynn Silbermann

Published by Game Changer Publishing

ISBN: 978-1-7370407-9-8

www.PublishABestSellingBook.com

DOWNLOAD YOUR FREE GIFTS

Read This First

Just to say thanks for buying and reading my book, I would like to give you a few free bonus gifts, no strings attached!

To Download Now, Visit

www.Divorce101.org/FreeGifts

I appreciate your interest in my book, and I value your feedback as it helps me improve future versions of this book. I would appreciate it if you could leave your invaluable review on Amazon.com with your feedback. Thank you!

The Straight Skinny
Divorce 101

Clarity Through Chaos

Jodi Lynn Silbermann

www.PublishABestSellingBook.com

TABLE OF CONTENTS

DEDICATION

This book is dedicated to John G. McGill, Jr., Attorney at Law. Thank you for always believing in me and helping me to believe in myself. The years of love and support you provided to both me and Ashley as a boss, a mentor, and most importantly, a friend will never be forgotten. The knowledge and wisdom you imparted to me over the years is immeasurable and lives on through me, my work, and this book. I would not be where I am today without having had you in my life. Thank you for my Wings!! J.G.M. Gave Me Wings; I learned how to fly!

INTRODUCTION

"Stepping onto a brand-new path is difficult, but not more difficult than remaining in a situation, which is not nurturing to the whole woman." -- **Maya Angelou**

There is so much more to divorce than the legal procedure. You've developed a life with someone else, and now that it's over, there can be a lot of confusion and pressure to make the best choices to secure your well-being and livelihood. My aim is to assist you in finding guidance amid the uncertainty to achieve the best possible results for yourself and any dependents who might be involved.

Take a deep breath. Inhale. Hold it for three seconds. Exhale. Congratulations, you've officially taken the first step towards success. If you're reading this sentence, it probably means that the 'divorce' process has made its way into your life in some shape or form. Maybe you're thinking about it, maybe you've decided on it, or maybe it's been decided for you.

Whatever the situation, maybe you're bound to have questions about what the future is about to look like. Some of those can't be answered, and that's okay, but some of those

3

questions, especially those about the legal process, can be answered, and this Guidebook is here to do just that. At some point in your life, you've probably heard the phrase "knowledge is power." While it is an astoundingly accurate statement in itself, it perhaps neglects to mention that knowledge is not always easily obtained.

If you were to open an internet browser and type in the word "divorce," it would give you approximately 546,000,000 results to choose from, which, to put it very simply, is a lot of information. But how many of those five hundred and forty-six million results are accurate or even helpful to you? Half? Twenty-five percent? It's almost impossible to say, but, for argument's sake, let's pick the figure of 0.0001%, giving us 546 results that were accurate and up to date. Out of those 546 results, how many of those would be written in a way that someone without a law degree could understand? Although the answer to that would vary from person to person, the fact remains that information, while being available, is not always accessible. That's what this book is looking to change.

Think of this book as a friend who not only has extensive and accurate knowledge of all things divorce-related but has made it their goal to help you through the legal process step by step. This friend is going to ensure that not only do you survive this process but that you go on to thrive. Now that may seem like a big promise to make, but after all, what are friends for?

How to Know If Hiring a Divorce Coach is Right For You?

You aren't looking for legal advice but you're feeling overwhelmed by the excessive paperwork and need help translating all of the "legal-speak" into a language that you can understand.

You know that choosing to exit your marriage is the right

thing to do but you're feeling stuck because you're not sure where to start and often feel waves of emotion that make it difficult to see a clear way forward.

You feel as if no one really understands what you're going through or the degree to which your divorce has impacted you personally and professionally.

You are seeking alternative legal services that can save you money and stress.

You no longer want to feel isolated and are seeking the support, expertise and guidance from someone who is empathetic and can help you successfully navigate both the legal and personal components of the divorce journey.

YOUR VOICE MATTERS

"The Voice. There is a voice inside of you That whispers all day long, 'I feel this is right for me. I know that this doesn't seem right.' No teacher, preacher, parent, friend Or wise man can decide what's right for you-- listen to the voice that speaks inside." - **Shel Silverstein**

No one goes into marriage planning to get divorced. You are probably feeling a cluster of different emotions; you may be wondering, "How did I get here?" Or you may know why you are here. As you begin to navigate the legal process, realize you know "***Your Story***" better than anyone else, and you know the outcome you desire to achieve more than anyone.

Whether you navigate the legal process represented by an attorney or representing yourself, remember that ***your voice matters***! A host of non-lawyer divorce professionals can support and guide you as you learn to advocate for yourself while navigating the divorce process. It is important to be an active participant in the divorce process so that you can achieve the best possible outcome for yourself.

You are your own best advocate!

Of course, you want to place yourself in the best possible situation to make rational and realistic decisions that serve your benefit, not only now but in the future. To become the best advocate you can be, you need to understand all that "stuff" that no one ever really explains.

- Do I need a lawyer?
- What are the steps involved in the divorce process?
- How long will it take until I am divorced?
- How do I pay my bills in the meantime?
- What does each step of the process entail?
- How can I best prepare myself for each step of the process?
- What are my attorney alternatives?
- How do I create an effective emotional support team?

In my professional experience, often, when a person feels divorce is imminent or they hear of someone dealing with divorce, the first thought is "I need to hire a lawyer," because there is a general misconception that because divorce involves a legal process, then one must have a lawyer. *Bzzzt, Wrong answer!* It is possible to get through the legal divorce process successfully without hiring an attorney. The courts have made it easy to meet the legal requirements by creating pre approved forms for each Stage of the process. As a matter of fact, as reported by Pro Se Statistics Reports in California alone, 80% of those that file the Petition for Divorce self-represented.

It's no secret that divorce and attorneys are expensive; according to an article in the U.S.A. Today, "...the average cost of divorce without children is $17,500.00". There are times during a divorce where attorney representation may be necessary; however, because of the excessive fees that go along with that option, more and more individuals are effectively navigating the legal process unrepresented—hiring an attorney may not always be the best strategy for several reasons. Throughout my career, I have witnessed amicable spouses become contentious due to attorney involvement. People tend to become guarded and defensive when an attorney enters the picture.

Because divorce involves a legal process, there tends to be a general assumption that an attorney must be retained to get through this process effectively. My boss referred to this as "Stinkin' Thinkin," I reference that term quite a bit throughout this Guidebook. Heed those "Stinkin' Thinkin'" warnings and learn from mistakes made by others who went through their divorce journey before you.

Not only are attorney's expensive, as you can see, in a case study by Harvard entitled *"Description of California Courts' Programs for Self-Represented Litigants..."* (Hough, Bonnie Rose, 2003) "California's courts are facing an ever-increasing number of litigants who go to court without legal counsel largely because they cannot afford representation."

The article goes on to say, "The growth of unrepresented litigants in family law is encouraging a re-thinking of how courts serve self-represented litigants throughout the system." As an observation, many of my clients had expressed that they received more latitude and better outcomes when they appeared in court on their behalf versus when an attorney represented them. The article further states, "In a similar study of case files from 1999, both parties were unrepresented in 75% of the cases...In only 11% of the cases were both parties represented." This Guidebook will help understand the purpose and role of an attorney and other types of professional divorce support services available and how to effectively utilize these services to help save money, time delays, and frustration along the way.

To achieve the best possible outcome for yourself, you **must** be an active, present, and participating member of your divorce team; remember, this is **YOUR** life! Statistics prove a majority of individuals involved in the legal divorce process are self-represented.

By taking you through the step-by-step stages of the divorce process, this Guidebook provides an ability to maintain a level of control and understanding to help empower you to advocate as you navigate the process.

Only YOU Know:

- What's best for yourself and your children (if you have them).
- What makes your spouse "tick."
- What went on behind closed doors.
- What outcome you desire to achieve.
- What your story is!

Without having a comprehensive understanding of the divorce process, it's very easy to be swept up and overwhelmed in the litany of legal paperwork, forms, blame games of "he said"/ "she said" only to find at the end of it, you're backed into a corner you don't want to be in and have no idea how to get out. Consistently, I hear clients represented by Attorneys complain because they feel their Attorney isn't doing anything. They are clueless about where they are in the process and have spent thousands of dollars just to feel helpless and unsure of how to proceed.

It is why it's so important to educate yourself; an attorney is not going to educate you about the legal process. In this process, sometimes things can move very quickly, and other times, it may seem as if nothing is happening. If you are informed and educated about the process and your options, you can advocate the direction of your divorce in a manner that helps achieve the best possible outcome.

I have noticed there is not much help out there for those

who want to advocate on their own behalf through the legal process.

You are your own best advocate; you know *your story* better than anyone else, and you care about the outcome more than anyone else will because you must live it.

MEET JODI

"Lack of clarity is the primary reason for failure in business and personal life." --**Brian Tracy, Peter Chee, 12 Disciplines of Leadership Excellence**

Behind every great Guidebook is its guide. Meet Jodi Silbermann, Founder, and C.E.O. of ***Just Call Jodi Incorporated*** and ***From We to Me***™, seasoned Paralegal, Divorce Coach and Manager, Registered Legal Document Assistant, and Author; she is an all-around Divorce Subject Matter Expert, servicing client divorce needs legally, emotionally and financially; from planning for divorce through planning the after divorce party and everything in between so they can go on to build a brighter future and grow ***From We to ME***! ™.

When it comes to navigating your way through the tumultuous divorce process, you could not find yourself in better hands. With thirty years experience as a legal professional Jodi already had the wisdom, knowledge, and skill set required to guide others successfully through a divorce; however, it would take a tragedy in her own life to propel her career to the next level.

No one knew that Jodi's marriage had been abusive for many years, she never talked to anyone about it. When her ex-husband finally got himself arrested for Domestic Violence, Jodi's boss, Attorney John G. McGill, Jr., took Jodi under his wing and helped guide her through some of the scariest times in her life.

At the height of Jodi's divorce, her boss, mentor, and friend of many years, suddenly passed away. It shook Jodi's foundation to its core. John's passing affected not only Jodi's professional life but her personal one as well; her boss had also been the attorney representing her in Court during her complicated divorce proceedings.

John was a Sole Practitioner, so despite the difficulties she was facing, Jodi took it upon herself to contact, arrange, and assist each client with transferring their file to a new attorney and closing the law practice operating for over 40 years.

It was an extremely scary and challenging time for Jodi. She had a strong support team that helped her find the courage and strength to tackle her biggest fear, standing up to her ex and represent herself against him, his attorney, and his team in Court. She did it! She faced them with direct and cross-examination, made sustainable objections, and had the Court admit her Exhibits as evidence in the Trial, and she WON her case!

Winning the case, she realized more than once she could identify with what many of her clients were experiencing and that is, no person should ever feel alone in their time of need. Her many years of legal experience combined with her personal experiences enabled her to quickly identify the void in Divorce Support for Women. She knew she was lucky enough to have the resources and knowledge of the legal process necessary to protect herself, but many women don't.

Jodi's fear became her passion, to inspire and empower

women through high-conflict relationship transitions so they can go on to be strong, confident, independent and create a brighter future for themselves. By providing support and guidance without judgment, Jodi's clients find a safe space in which they can take back control of their own lives and create the foundation for a better future. This book takes that mantra and uses it to guide you on your journey towards independence, empowerment, and ultimately: happiness.

You can easily Contact Jodi incorporated on social media

https://www.facebook.com/justcalljodi
https://www.linkedin.com/in/justcalljodiinc/
justcalljodi.org

MY MISSION

My mission is to provide you with specific tools, education, and a framework to empower you with the knowledge and confidence to make informed decisions at every stage of the divorce process. When you choose *Just Call Jodi Incorporated*, the focus isn't on IF you will survive, it's really a question of how healthy, whole and transformed you want to BE once you make your transformation ***From We to ME***™?

QUICK GUIDE

"A season of loneliness and isolation is when the caterpillar gets its wings.

Remember that the next time you feel alone." - **Mandy Hale**

Divorce is a process. It's a legal process. It's a financial process, but the worst and hardest part is it's an emotional process. My mission with this guidebook is to empow**HER** women with the ability to maintain a level of control and make informed decisions at every stage of the legal process; to ensure you are protected in the present and ready to prosper in the future by providing:

- Tips
- Tools
- Education
- Knowledge
- Wisdom
- Framework

I won't promise it will be easy because it won't be, but it

WILL be worth it, that I can promise. I have lived more life in my 7 1/2 years as an independent woman than I did in my 23 years in marriage captivity.

On my own, I was able to see my daughter off to college, purchased my own home, earn my BA in Business Administration and my TESOL Certification to teach English overseas. I used it when I traveled to Thailand for 3 months to teach English at a camp for Korean children. And, most important, I Founded, *Call Jodi Incorporated* and *From We to Me*™, so I can continue helping women effectively navigate through their high-conflict divorce challenges.

My worst days are better than my best days were when I was married. They may be bad days, but they are my bad days. No matter where you are in life, there will always be good and bad; what you do with them and how you handle them makes the difference in how bright you build your future.

I believe we are each our own best advocates in life. You know **Your Story** better than anyone else does, AND you care about the outcome of **Your Story** more than any third-party person ever will.

A friend once said, "Life is either blessin's or lessons" and I believe divorce is a combination of both.

Be proud of yourself, reading and using this book, you have already taken steps toward:

- ✔ Success
- ✔ Becoming your own best advocate
- ✔ Building your own brighter future
- ✔ Empowering yourself
- ✔ Taking control of a life-changing situation
- ✔ Educating yourself about the process

- ✔ Seeking command over your life

- ✔ Exploring your options

- ✔ Winning the battle over fear.

My passion is helping women transition through high-conflict divorces and domestic violence situations. It makes me think there is a huge misconception and lack of understanding about what constitutes domestic violence and how it works. Even amongst the legal community, attorneys, the courts, the legal system, and the police, there is just a general lack of education on this topic. For me, my advocate was everything. I work in the legal system, and I still had to ask questions, so I understand someone who doesn't have my experience or access; it's a scary thing because nobody listens, and the system is not designed to recognize it. That's really where *Just Call Jodi Incorporated* comes in; I created a place to help women find their voice, use their voice and use it effectively so people will hear them, understand the insidious nature of abuse and how it works so that they can get through to the authorities and the court; to effectively protect themselves. At *Just Call Jodi Incorporated,* we educate women on advocating for themselves because it's you who has to do it. We teach you how to grow *From We to ME*™, the rest is up to you.

HOW TO USE THIS GUIDE

"Sometimes, it's the smallest decisions that can change your life forever." -- **Keri Russell**

I realize no one has the time, nor desire, to read yet another "self-help" book! That's why this is more of a Guidebook and not meant for you to have read it from cover to cover. This Guidebook takes you step-by-step through the legal process, the related forms, and proper court procedures from start to finish. The Guidebook is divided into 3 parts, **the Beginning, the Middle,** and **the New Beginning-Growing From We to ME™,** so that you can go directly to the subject matter or topic related to your current situation. My purpose with this Guidebook is to provide individuals experiencing the divorce process with:

Step-by-Step Overviews	Practical Tips and Tools
Simplified Easy to Understand Explanations	Knowledge
Coaching Insight	Personal Strategy
Helpful Worksheets	and more...

I created this Guidebook and *The Straight Skinny ~ Divorce 101 Program*, as a means of guiding you through this perplexing process and as a way to provide clarification, perspective, comprehension, and concentration to an overwhelming process.

I'm in a unique position, and have personal and professional experience in all aspects of divorce, the legal process, and the court system. There are thousands of self-help books out there that help people with the emotional side of the divorce process; very few break down the legal process or describe how to navigate through the process in a way that is simple, easy to understand, or really at all.

My goal with this Guidebook is to empower women to advocate for themselves through the legal process of divorce and seek the appropriate support, expertise, and guidance. Find support professionals who are empathetic and can help effectively navigate the legal and personal components involved in the divorce journey.

PART ONE

The Beginning

"I believe in being strong when everything seems to be going wrong. I believe that happy girls are the prettiest girls. I believe that tomorrow is another day, and I believe in miracles." -- **Audrey Hepburn**

CHAPTER ONE

GAINING CLARITY THROUGH CHAOS

"There are things in my life that are hard to reconcile, like divorce. Sometimes it is very difficult to make sense of how it could happen. Blame is so easy. I don't have time for hate or negativity in my life. There's no reason. There's no room for it." - **Reese Witherspoon**

I'm going to assume you're reading this book because of an impending divorce; no matter which spouse decided to initiate the divorce, it's critical to make some important, educated, and informed decisions for yourself as you prepare for the road ahead of you. While the legal process is straightforward, the emotions that go along with the process are not! The emotions are what makes this process so complicated and attorney fees so outrageous.

"When one door closes, another opens; but we always look so long and regretfully at the closed door that we miss the open ones" -- **Alexander Graham Bell.**

When I ask divorced women, "What do you think you'll

benefit from this?" I'm usually met with blank stares and silence. But, after a brief pause, I usually see a sparkle in their eyes when they say, in some form or another, "I'll get **ME** back."

Yes, exactly! This is the sense of self that many people discover after they divorce. I chose the word "evolve" because as you go through life and grow, new joys, fulfillment, and all kinds of possibilities emerge. Sure, there would be some difficulties along the way. But you can't evolve if you don't face challenges head-on, work your way through them, and keep striving for your full potential!

So, no matter what stage of divorce you are in, whether you are just thinking about it, in the middle of it, or several years out, your goal should be to find yourself again and become everything you want to be.

Now that the relationship is over, there can be a tremendous amount of uncertainty and pressure to make the right decisions to protect the well-being, you and any children you may have. Are you getting it? Now, let's continue.

Fear and emotions are on overdrive for both of you, making this a volatile time in your life; you are each probably experiencing some degree of hurt or angry causing one or the other of you to lash out; causing a reaction that puts both of you into an angry tail-spin of finger-pointing, blaming, name-calling, etc. It is a merry-go-round you don't want to ride. Later in this book, I provide some Tips & Tools to help avoid toxic communications.

Your spouse may be behaving in a way that has you thinking to yourself, "Who the hell is this person?", "This is not the person I married." Don't be shocked when the sweetest of sweet, nicest of nice, and the most loving person you married, no matter what they may have said in the past, has suddenly become someone you just don't recognize. They are hostile, angry, and completely uncaring of you or your feelings. Even

26

under the most amicable divorce circumstances, feelings of hurt, disappointment, failure, jealousy, distrust, and fear still tend to rear their ugly face.

Conversely, when dealing with a high-conflict spouse, they most likely already exhibited or engaged in abusive, toxic, and some form of destructive behavior during the marriage. It's quite characteristic for those same bad behaviors to continue and often escalate as the divorce process progresses.

Identifying and protecting yourself from a high-conflict spouse is very important and discussed in greater detail in further Chapters of this Guidebook.

It is important to be mindful when you speak to your spouse; think before you speak; be mindful of the tone in which the message is delivered. It is not always what is said but *how* it is conveyed causing an argument or an important message to be lost in delivery.

- You may currently react negatively to each other.
- You may each have conflicting reasons/versions for the underlying emotions or feelings (anger, hurt, sadness, etc.) that may have been a factor in the demise of your marriage.
- You each know exactly "which button to push" to hurt one another.
- Your spouse may use your insecurities as a weapon to get a reaction or rise out of you, to keep you off balance. It is common when dealing with a high-conflict spouse.

Always remain on the high road during your divorce journey and forge ahead with a positive attitude, as much as you can. Don't engage in useless name-calling or blame games; focus on building that brighter future that's right in front of you.

As hard as it will be at times, it is so important to remain the bigger person and stay on that high road; *even*, when you know you are so mad or upset that everything in you wants to get into the mud pit and sling mud right back in your spouse's face. Someone must be the bigger person and the voice of reason, so why not let it be you!

I am well aware of how difficult it is at times to take that high; I also know the high road can feel very isolated and lonely at times; but look at it this way; on the high road, there isn't much traffic, you never get pulled over, and there is never any reason to question your driving ability.

Emotions are the largest part of the divorce process; however, the legal forum is **NOT** the place to address these emotions. That's the time to check your emotions at the door. In a later Chapter this Guidebook discusses options for divorce support professionals to help deal with divorce, emotions and getting through the process.

When you're dealing with the legal part of the divorce process; look at it with the same perspective as someone dealing with a business transaction; fundamentally, that's what the legal process of Divorce is; the dissolving of a partnership, the partnership known as Marriage. Hence, the name of the legal process ~ "Dissolution of Marriage" ~.

Follow the basic principles discussed throughout this Guidebook, put forth the effort, work on your mindset, follow an action plan and surround yourself with the appropriate support team; you WILL thrive as you successfully navigate the divorce process, I promise.

CHAPTER TWO

AVOID THE GALLOPING "WHAT-IF'S…"

"Fear defeats more people than any other one thing in the world." -- **Ralph Waldo Emerson**

Before we get into the nuts and bolts of the process, I want to caution you that it's time to start to reign in and re-focus those runaway thoughts that tend to have us "what-if…" every crazy little nuance and outlandish possibility. There's that "Stinkin' Thinkin'," and it's time to stop!

Constantly thinking "what-if…" will only serve to drive your friends, family, your support team, and yourself bonkers and get you nowhere.

As a trained legal divorce professional, I, too, had those moments when I would turn to my boss, just for some reassurance that those same answers I provide to clients every day also apply to me. Everyone thinks their story is different; trust me, it isn't that different. While the underlying specifics may be different, the mechanics of divorce are the same for everyone. The significant variables in the divorce process are the names, faces, circumstances, and individual perceptions.

Like life, there is no possible way to develop a solution for every scenario that may arise in the future. Some things will have to be addressed when and if it happens.

Remember, you're probably already living the "worst-case scenario." For the most part, there is a legal remedy for just about any of the "What if..." situations that have already or will cross your mind. The reality is that chances are slim to none that most of the scenarios you are conjuring in your mind will ever come to fruition.

Some Common "What If's..."

- What if he does quit his job as he threatened?
- What if he is trying to hide money or transfer property?
- What if he won't settle?
- What if I don't get the support I need?
- What if we have to sell the house?
- What if he refuses to give me any money?
- What if he leaves the country with our children?
- What if he avoids being served?

Patience "Grasshopper"!! Your divorce journey will require a lot of it!

CHAPTER THREE

CHECK EMOTIONS AT THE DOOR

"It always gets worse before it can get better. But it will get better. Like everything else, and like our past struggles, at some point, we win, but before that win, there's always that loss that spurs us on."—
Dolores Huertahttps

It may be the first time you are dealing with any legal process; I realize anything that involves the Courts can be daunting, especially when you are unfamiliar with how the law and the process work.

I'm going to share a secret, the legal part of the divorce process is the simple part; honestly, it is!

Divorce is only as complicated as the people involved want it to be!

As was mentioned at the beginning of this Guidebook, from a strictly legal perspective, divorce is the breakdown, liquidation, and division of a business partnership, known to us as *"marriage"*.

Because emotions tend to cloud judgment, approach your divorce with a business transaction mindset, removing emotion from your reactions and decisions. I realize this is much easier said than done. It also does not mean ignoring your emotions; it just means dealing with them in a different forum, not the legal forum.

Recognize your own 'danger zone.' Your risk zone is the area of your life where you are susceptible to impulsive behavior and emotional outbursts. When you start paying attention to your body's signals, you'll know this reaction and be able to take steps to avoid going there. When my stomach tightens, my pulse races, my neck tenses, and my breathing becomes shallow, I know I'm in danger. A fluttering feeling pervades my whole body. I'm aware that I'm emotionally reactive, and I'm afraid I'll soon say or do things I'll come to regret. If I let my emotions take over and respond reactively to the situation, I will not be making conscious decisions about my behavior. Difficulties are just around the corner!

Allow me to give you an example. When I walk into my daughter's room, it is in complete disarray. I've asked her many times to keep it clean, but here I am once again confronted with a virtual pigsty. I have a feeling I'm going to burst. So, what should I do? Do I let loose and wreak more havoc, or do I flee? I turn and walk away. I leave for three minutes to do some deep breathing and to calm myself down. Maybe I'll go for a quick walk around the corner. I calm down and now have the ability to make a very deliberate decision about how I want to approach the situation. The keyword here is 'conscious choice.' Only conscious choice exists, whereas being reactive is unconscious. I decide to return and have a fair discussion that will result in specific consequences if she does not follow any simple house rules.

Over a week, you will face hundreds of decisions, ranging from bonding with your children to making decisions about the divorce and your future. Being emotionally reactive is a choice. The choice is the result of conscious thought, which means you must control your emotions. When you see a reactive reaction emerging, take a step back, calm down, and then and only then choose.

Both personally and professionally, I like to apply the K.I.S.S. methodology; Keep It Simple Stupid. Sometimes, it's necessary to take a more linear approach to things; dealing with the legal system is one time.

Fear and emotion are a normal part of this process; they are also the most complicated and chaotic part of the divorce process. The purpose of the court is not to confirm that your soon-to-be-ex is an A** H**e, even if they are!

The legal system has no place for **EMOTION**. The legal system operates solely on law and evidence, NOT emotion!

> *When you are dealing with the legal side of your divorce,*
>
> *you MUST check your emotions at the door.*

As you begin to experience the roller coaster of emotions, often a natural part of a divorce, I strongly caution against solely relying on your friends and family as your support system. While they may mean well, they tend to give inaccurate information, causing unnecessary and added stress; rather than helping to mitigate the level of stress, it increases it.

While each divorce is unique and has its own set of circumstances; the mechanics and the process is always the same. For instance, just because your friend Mary is getting $10,000 a month in "support," that doesn't mean you're going to get $10,000 a month in support. You have no idea how they arrived at the amount, or the financial intricacies of Mary's marriage. Maybe Mary's husband earned a six-figure plus salary, and your husband is earning $50,000 a year, or he's a lazy a** and just chose not to work at all, which I experienced in my divorce.

When dealing with the emotional side of divorce, it may be helpful to engage the services of qualified divorce support professionals for support and guidance. The legal system, including attorneys, is not intended to address the emotions that are a natural part of this process.

CHAPTER FOUR

THE PROCESS IN A NUTSHELL

"...By good rights, I ought not to have so much put on me, but there seems no other way. Len says one steady pull more ought to do it. He says the best way out is always through. And I agree to that, or in so far as that I can see no way out but through— Leastways for me..." **(Frost, Robert, 1915, Servants of Servant Poem)**

People successfully navigate the court system without an attorney every day. Did you know...

"Over 4.3 million court users are self-represented in California." (Pro Se Statistics, 2017)

When it comes to divorce, "...80% of petitioners at disposition for dissolution cases are self-represented." (Pro Se Statistics, Compiled by Madelynn Herman, National Center for State Courts, June 21, 2006)

Some of the most contentious divorce cases are often

settled in the courthouse hallways before anyone even makes it into the courtroom to see the judge. According to, *2017 Court Statistics Report*, most divorce cases reach an agreement at some point in the process, "... less than 1% of divorce cases are disposed of at trial."

The legal process of divorce; is a fairly straight forward, forms, driven process. It is the **people, emotions,** and sometimes the attorneys that complicate and stall the process. The process is not rocket science, and it isn't overly complicated; you don't need the Degree, or need to be a lawyer to advocate for yourself, or represent yourself through the legal process.

Understanding the flow of the legal process and what's involved at each stage will help prepare and organize you to become the best advocate for yourself.

This Guidebook contains a Divorce Case Roadmap that gives a big-picture overview of the 3 stages involved in the legal divorce process. This Guidebook walks through each stage of the process step-by-step and translates "legal-speak" to make it easier to understand.

Now it's time to dive right in. If you didn't know, all family law forms start with the letters "F.L." followed by the form number. Be sure to use the most recent version of the form; the form number and publication date are located on the bottom left-hand corner of each form. The right-hand corner indicates the California Family Court Code Section for that legal form. You can then look up the Family Code Section referenced and read about the California law that pertains to that specific form.

Again, this Guidebook is based on California law and procedure; always check the laws, court rules and procedures, for your city, county, and state, before filing any paperwork with the Court.

Let's start with some basic information and understanding about starting a Divorce:

How do I know which Courthouse to use?

1. Residency Requirements

The Courthouse jurisdiction is determined by the residency of either the Petitioner or the Respondent. In California, to establish legal residency, one must live in the State of California for a minimum of 6 months and in the county of filing for a minimum of 3 months. Each state has its laws, which may differ from California, so be sure to confirm the local laws for your City, County, and State.

2. California is referred to as a "no-fault" state. What does that mean?

- Neither spouse must prove that the other party is "at fault" as a reason for divorce.
- The choices as the reason for the divorce: "irreconcilable differences" or "permanent legal incapacity to make decisions."
- The court is not interested in hearing about any other cause for the divorce.
- The court is not interested in hearing about any extra-marital affairs.
- The court is not interested in the transgressions of either person.
- California is a "Community Property" state. What does that mean?
- Anything that was acquired during the time you were married. In short, any income earned or debt incurred, by either or both of you, from the Date of Marriage through the Date of Separation.

3. What is considered as "Separate Property"?

- Income earned or debt incurred on or after the date of separation.
- Any property owned before marriage.
- Any property received during the marriage as a gift or inheritance.

4. Four main components are involved in a divorce.

- KIDS = Child Custody, Visitation, Parenting, and Co-Parenting.
- MONEY = Child Support and Spousal Support.
- PROPERTY DIVISION = marital assets, debts, household furniture, and furnishings.
- DATE OF SEPARATION = The last day the parties considered themselves living together as husband and wife.

5. This Guidebook has broken down the divorce process into 3 Stages:

- Stage 1 – Initial Filing (Personal Service & Response).
- Stage 2 – Financial Disclosures (& Discovery, if necessary).
- Stage 3 – Final Judgment – Settlement Agreement or Trial.

The road to **Stage 3** and getting that, *Final Judgment*, wholly depends on the 2 people involved in the divorce. An amicable couple will arrive at Stage **3,** *Final Judgment*, quicker and smoother than a high-conflict couple. This road will be bumpy and windy but eventually you will arrive, either by a Settlement Agreement or a Court Trial, where a Judge will make all final decisions on the terms and conditions of the **Final Judgment**. Later in this Guidebook is a Chapter that takes a deeper look into understanding the difference between an amicable spouse and a high conflict spouse.

Flowchart of the Stages in the Divorce Process.

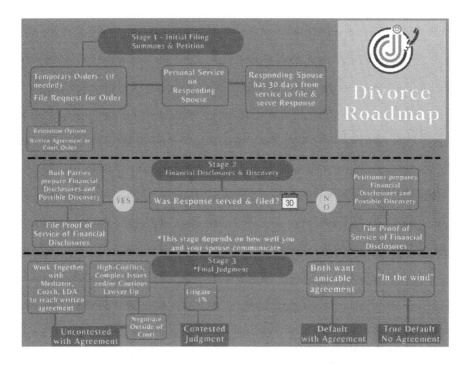

CHAPTER FIVE

IDENTIFYING AND GATHERING FINANCIAL DOCUMENTS

"Out of clutter, find simplicity. From discord, find harmony. In the middle of difficulty lies opportunity." -- **Albert Einstein**

To advocate for your interests and needs, you need to know what you're working with to get the best possible outcome. It's time to get started with some of the "heavy liftings," so it's out of the way when the time comes. It will help you handle the financial situation you face, avoid delays and keep the divorce moving along.

The marital finances are a big deal and a large source of contention when couples are divorcing. As a Divorce Subject Matter Expert, it has been my experience that the topic of money can make even the most amicable couples argue. I have found, high-conflict men, in particular, tend to become very controlling when it comes to money. Money is used as a tool for control, forcing settlement by the other party to circumvent the financial disclosure process and rush the process.

There is a requirement for each spouse in California to exchange honest and accurate *financial disclosure* information. If you and your spouse can work together, you may work on these forms together. That strategy won't work in cases that involve a high-conflict spouse.

The *financial disclosure* process cannot and should not be circumvented. The Court will not allow a Judgment to be entered if the parties fail to file proof with the Court that *financial disclosures* have been properly served by each spouse, as set forth by law.

To assist in identifying various financial documents that may be required, a checklist and worksheets are included at the end of this chapter. Suppose there is available access to any of the financial records and statements. In that case, it's a good idea to make copies and store those records at an offsite location with a friend, family member, or other trusted source. There may be additional financial documentation requested that is not included in this list.

The financial documents are a critical part of the divorce process, and they provide a snapshot of what the 2 of you owed and owned as of the date of separation. The *financial disclosures* are used as a roadmap when the time comes to negotiate a fair and amicable settlement. With a high-conflict spouse, accessing the appropriate financial documentation and information can sometimes be difficult, particularly when the other party is generally uncooperative. Often a high conflict spouse will withhold financial documents to control the situation or hide something shady they may have done.

Don't panic if you cannot find all of the financial documents right away.

There are many reasons why you may not have access to some or all the financial documents.

Maybe...

- You have no clue where the documents are.
- You're unable to access them.
- You're just not able to find all of them.
- Your spouse is withholding them.
- You never had access to them.
- You just have no clue what any of your financial matters are.

If the other spouse is just blatantly delaying completion of the Preliminary Financial Disclosures, providing incomplete or inaccurate information, or just straight playing bull**it games, there may be a need to seek legal advice on using the legal process known as "Discovery." This Guidebook explores a little bit about the "Discovery" process.

As the divorce progresses, it can sometimes become more difficult to promptly get your hands on certain financial documents; getting a jump start will help avoid frustration and possibly long, costly delays.

As a tool to help as you advocate through the **financial disclosure** part of the process, this Guidebook contains the following *Checklists and Worksheets* to help keep you organized as you begin to gather information and documentation.

Checklists and Worksheets

- A checklist of things you can do to prepare for Divorce;
- A comprehensive list of common financial documents you can begin to gather; and
- A worksheet you can begin a list:
  - Marital Assets

- Marital Debts
- Marital Income
- Marital Expenses
- Separate Property
- Any other important financial information you may want to jot down or need to follow up about.

When the time comes, you will be prepared and ready to advocate for yourself!

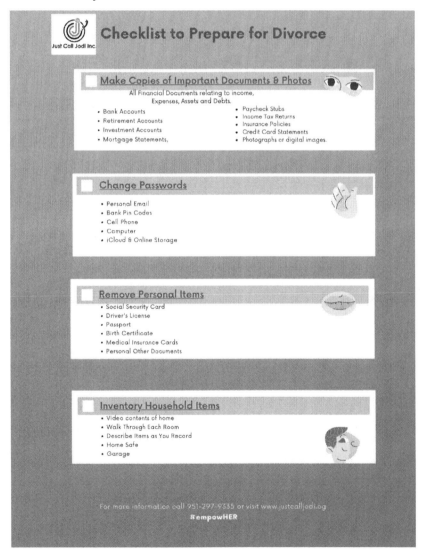

CHECKLIST OF FINANCIAL DOCUMENTS

Tax Return for the past three (3) years	Personal
Business if applicable	Proof of Current Income – gather pay stubs for the last two months for each party
If self-employed, a Profit and Loss Statement or recent Schedule C	Banking Information
Checking Account Statements	Savings Account Statements
Certificate of Deposit Statements	Debt Information
Credit Card Statements	Loan Statements
Mortgage Loan Statement	Auto Loan Statement
HELOC Statement	Personal Loan Statement
Business Loan Statement	Investment Accounts
Stocks	Bonds
Mutual Funds	Retirement Accounts
I.R.A.'s	Pensions
401(k)	Profit Sharing
Annuities	Deferred Compensation, etc.
Life Insurance	Declaration page for any Life Insurance with cash surrender or loan value
Real Property	Title Deeds
Property Tax Statements	Insurance
Auto Insurance	Homeowners Insurance
Medial Insurance	Title Documents for Vehicles, Boats, Trailers
Itemized listing of Household, Furniture, Furnishings, and Appliances	Itemized listing of Jewelry, Antiques, Coin Collections, etc.
Business Records	Profit & Loss Statements
Copies of any accounts receivables or unsecured notes	Recent Schedule C or form K-1 for partnerships or business interests
Separate Property	Any property documents purchased before marriage or received by way of inheritance.
Prenuptial or Postnuptial Agreements	Estate Planning Documents – Wills or Trusts

DIVORCE BRAINSTORMING WORKSHEET

State of residence for past 6 months:

County of residence for past 3 months:

Tax Refund
☐ N/A

Life Insurance
☐ N/A

Investments
☐ N/A

Retirement Plans
☐ N/A

Partnerships or other Business Interests
☐ N/A

Other Assets
☐ N/A

DIVORCE BRAINSTORMING WORKSHEET

Do you want to restore your former name: (YES) OR (NO)

If yes, what is your former name:

Credit Cards
☐ N/A

Loans - Secured and Unsecured
☐ N/A

Student Loans
☐ N/A

Taxes Owed
☐ N/A

Other Debts
☐ N/A

Concerns
☐ N/A

DIVORCE BRAINSTROMING WORKSHEET

Do you think you will need an
order for support: YES OR NO

Are you dealing with a high-
conflict spouse?   YES OR NO

Your Current Monthly Income	Your Spouses Current Monthly Income
☐ N/A	☐ N/A

Investment Income	Other Souces of Income for either of you
☐ N/A	☐ N/A

Health Insurance	Health Costs Not Covered by Insurance
☐ N/A	☐ N/A

DIVORCE BRAINSTORMING WORKSHEET

Will you need to get health
insurance; once divorce is final?   (YES) OR (NO)

Which spouse has typically been
the higher wage earner?

Monthly Expense for Home

- [ ] N/A
- [ ] Mortgage _____
- [ ] Rent   _____

Monthly Child Care Expenses

- [ ] N/A

Monthly Grocery & household Supplies

- [ ] N/A

Monthly Cost for Eating Out

- [ ] N/A

Monthly Utility Expenses

- [ ] N/A
- [ ] Gas   _____
- [ ] Electricity _____
- [ ] Water   _____
- [ ] Trash   _____
- [ ] Other   _____

Monthly Expense for Telephone

- [ ] N/A
- [ ] Cellphone   _____
- [ ] Landline   _____
- [ ] Email   _____
- [ ] Wi-fi   _____
- [ ] Other   _____

49

DIVORCE BRAINSTORMING WORKSHEET

Is someone currently helping you pay your monthly expenses? If so, how much?   (YES) OR (NO) _____

Are there minor children, If yes, how many?   (YES) OR (NO) _____

Monthly Expenses for Laundry & Cleaning	Monthly Expenses for Clothes
☐ N/A	☐ N/A
☐ Mortgage _____	
☐ Rent _____	

Monthly Expenses for Education	Monthly Expenses for Entertainment. Gifts & Vacations
☐ N/A	☐ N/A

Monthly Auto & Transportation Expense	Monthly Expense for Insurance Policies
☐ N/A	☐ N/A _____
☐ Insurance _____	☐ Life _____
☐ Gas _____	☐ Accident _____
☐ Repairs _____	☐ Auto _____
☐ Bus _____	☐ Renters _____
☐ Etc. _____	☐ Home _____

Just Call Jodi Incorporated
From We to Me™
Telephone: 951-297-9335
Email: info@justcalljodiinc.com
Website: justcalljodi.org

CHAPTER SIX

UNDERSTANDING THE DIFFERENCE BETWEEN THE AMICABLE SPOUSE AND THE HIGH CONFLICT SPOUSE

"Bad divorce?" Hardy asked, his gaze falling to my hands. I realized I was clutching my purse in a death grip. "No, the divorce was great," I said. "It was the a marriage that sucked." ~ **Lisa Kleypas, Blue-Eyed Devil**

Most divorces involve some level of contention, conflict and a heightened sense of emotion and possible distrust over certain issues. Most of the time, it's over financial issues and children.

When dealing with an amicable spouse, ultimately, both sides are fairly reasonable and eventually able to set aside their differences and hurt feelings; work together to reach an amicable solution in the best interest of all the parties.

The amicable spouse is not interested in creating a constant state of war against the other spouse. Both people learn to communicate effectively with one another, co-parent without intentionally trying to hurt the other person, or using the children as weapons.

When changes in the children's schedule happen, which I guarantee they will, the amicable spouse can easily adapt to these changes and work together to reach a solution.

When the parties are amicable, they can work together, reach a fair and equitable agreement, and the best part, nobody ever even sees the inside of a courtroom. On the flip side, there's the high conflict spouse that lives in a constant state of war, causes intentionally continued conflict, and tries to upset you out of anger and spite.

Chances are you already know or have an idea if your spouse is in high-conflict. Past behavior is probably the best indication of how they will behave during the divorce process.

When dealing with a high-conflict spouse, it's important to prepare yourself as much as possible. The safety of you and your children, if any, is the foremost priority.

Common threats you may hear from a high-conflict spouse:

"You'll never see the kids again."	"The money's mine, and you won't see a dime."
"I will take the kids, leave the country, and you'll never see them again."	"I will tell the courts you are an unfit mother.."
Large withdrawals of cash or other assets	"This is my house, and you have to leave."
"A restraining order is a piece of paper and cannot stop a bullet."	"You will have no money to hire an attorney."
"You have to do what I'm telling you to do or you will end up with nothing."	"Take what I'm giving you or get nothing at all."
"You will be sorry," Attempts to try and force you to accept a settlement that is not in your best interest as a way to try and get around the legal obligation of full disclosure of financial documents in particularly when they're hiding something.	I will quit my job, and you will never see a dime of support."

A tip my boss taught me, "Generally, those who threaten don't!" It is a bully tactic used to manipulate someone with the use of fear. The high-conflict spouse often exhibits some form of controlling and narcissistic traits. A high-conflict spouse will often make you feel or believe:

- You are the problem.
- You are the reason for the divorce.
- You are crazy.
- You are not enough as a wife and mother.
- Your weaknesses and insecurities are used against

you as a weapon.

These behaviors are all about manipulation and control—period end of the story.

Have you ever heard the word "gaslighting."? It is one of the first terms I educate clients about when dealing with a high-conflict spouse. Understanding what gaslighting is and how it works has helped my clients regain their power as they more easily identify the manipulation and control tactics used by their spouse.

As a survivor myself, I too experienced gaslighting. My advocate educated me about the term, gaslighting and it immediately resonated with me. Since then, I have found that gaslighting is a common form of abuse that most of my clients dealing with a high-conflict spouse have experienced.

Working with the support of a Divorce Coach, L.M.F.T., Counselor, Therapist, or some other Divorce Support Professional experienced in dealing with high-conflict divorce may educate you and help you to remain strong as you continue to advocate through the process.

Psychology Today describes gaslighting as "An insidious form of manipulation and psychological control. Victims of gaslighting are deliberately and systematically fed false information. That leads them to question what they know to be true often about themselves. They may end up doubting their memory, their perception, and even their sanity. Over time, a gaslighters' manipulations can grow more complex and potent, making it increasingly difficult for the victim to see the truth."

Domestic Violence

"For that morning when you wake up and realize it's going to be OK, And then the dream dies, and the dream breaks into a tiny million pieces which leaves

you with a choice. You can either stick with it (which is unbearable), or you can go off and dream another dream." — **Rachel (Meryl Streep) in Heartburn**

Domestic violence in any form should be taken very seriously. The safety of you and your children is the NUMBER ONE PRIORITY, above all else. If you are currently in danger or fear for yourself and your children's safety, please immediately call the national domestic violence hotline 1-800-799-SAFE (7233) and contact a Lawyer or Legal Document Assistant about seeking a Domestic Violence Restraining Order.

The statistics on domestic violence is alarming. I bet you will be surprised to learn, on average, "1 in 4 women experience **severe** intimate partner abuse that has resulted in some form of injury; 1 in 3 women experience some form of domestic violence." (ncadv.org/STATISTICS) If that's not a pandemic, then I don't know what is. Look around you, 1 in 3 women that equates to just about everybody.

Many women don't understand, acknowledge or even realize they are the victim of domestic violence. It's this dirty little secret no one ever wants to talk about. There is a stigma of guilt and shame still attached to it and generally not discussed during water cooler conversation.

Society has been trained to believe that some forms of abuse are acceptable and that abuse is black eyes and bloody noses like we see in television movies. That's just more "Stinkin' Thinkin'"!!

Abuse comes in many forms:

- Verbal
- Emotional
- Financial
- Physical
- Sexual

I'm sure there are many other forms not mentioned here, as well.

"Close to 20 people per minute are abused by an intimate partner in the United States, equating to more than 10 million men and women.",

(ncadv.org/STATISTICS)

The common denominator in all forms of abuse is = **Control**.

In my experience as a divorce professional, when an abuser begins to lose control over the victim, they become angry, irrational, and many times dangerous and unpredictable. This behavior is scary and can become dangerous and prevents many women from leaving, and often is what forces them to return.

If you're experiencing some form of domestic violence abuse, you may need to consider seeking a domestic violence restraining order to protect yourself and your children. Again, the safety of you and your children is always your number 1 priority. Statistics reflect that domestic violence is a growing problem that affects women and men worldwide, from all walks of life.

California does have laws to help protect individuals experiencing domestic violence, which includes verbal and emotional abuse. So, in other words, if your spouse yells at you and calls you vial names, that IS verbal abuse!

A common trait when dealing with the high-conflict spouse, they can be verbally and emotionally abusive. It is important to recognize that just because someone didn't hit you; DOES NOT mean it's not abuse. As a form of abuse, verbal abuse tends to be more damaging than physical abuse; it leaves far deeper scars than and takes much longer to heal, if ever for some.

From personal and professional experience, dealing with

domestic violence issues is where the biggest defect in our "justice" system occurs. I have found, when it comes to abuse, the *system* itself (which includes Courts, attorneys, police, and the laws) tends to have a general lack of education, knowledge, and understanding as to the insidious nature of abuse and how it works. Suppose you are dealing with an abusive spouse. In that case, it is important to seek a divorce support professional that understands the dynamics of Domestic Violence and the legal system to ensure you protect and properly advocate for yourself as you navigate this bumpy, windy road.

If you have experienced any form of abuse during your marriage, seek the appropriate recovery method, allow yourself the time you need to heal and, surround yourself with a strong divorce support team, recognize you are enough, and most importantly, that it's not your fault. You need to know these things as you move forward in this process dealing with a high-conflict spouse.

Common Patterns of Behavior

Harassment	Cyber-stalking
Disparaging remarks disparaging you to your children, friends, family, or those close to you.	Threatening messages.
Declarations of controlling the divorce process.	Attempt to control finances or hide Assets.
Refusal to communicate.	Hiding of unknown assets or money.
Refusing to co-parent or co-parent Effectively.	Stalking and cyberstalking on social media, texting.

Emergency Plan

Pack a safety bag and find a safe a place to hide it.	Determine who your safe people are.
Stash some cash away.	Protect your privacy.
Put in safekeeping all documents, keepsakes, and jewelry.	Contact divorce support professional or domestic violence shelter for help.
Get a domestic violence restraining Order.	
Get a domestic violence restraining order.	Go no contact - disengaged with the other Party.
Set aside as much cash as you can.	Remove yourself from all social media Platforms.
Change your phone number.	Stop communicating with mutual third party, friends, and family that are communicating back and forth between the two of you.
Keep a log of all incidents, dates, and times. Be as detailed as you possibly can and report whatever you can to the authorities about the refusal by your ex to cooperate in the divorce process.	

Safety tips

You can follow a few general rules when dealing with a high-conflict spouse that may help you not lose your mind as you navigate some of the twists and turns that will inevitably occur along the road of divorce.

- Imagine you are wearing a Teflon; keep it handy; you're going to need it.
- Always remain on the high road.
- Keep a written log of specific dates, times, and details of bad behavior.
- Communicate and confirm everything in writing.
- Avoid personal interactions.
- Be proactive, don't count on your ex to handle things you know they won't.
- Respond only when necessary and don't antagonize the situation.
- Don't try to get them to see the error in their ways – it won't happen.
- DO NOT expect the legal system, a lawyer, a judge, or the process will change your spouse, and it won't!

Accepting a few of these pains now will save you a ton of future aggravation, headaches, and sleepless nights.

CHAPTER SEVEN

STAGE 1 – STARTING THE LEGAL PROCESS

"Divorce isn't such a tragedy. A tragedy's staying in an unhappy marriage, teaching your children the wrong things about love. Nobody ever died of divorce." – **Jennifer Weiner**

Now that we've established what you can do to prepare, protect and advocate for yourself as you begin to move forward through the divorce process. It is a good time to start surrounding yourself with a strong support team.

Many attorneys offer free consultations. As a way to educate yourself, make a comprehensive list of questions, book a free consultation with an attorney, or several if necessary, ask as many questions as they will answer until you feel your questions and concerns have been adequately addressed as you start to advocate through the process.

Strategy Tidbit

> *Once you or your spouse consults with an attorney about the divorce matter, the other spouse cannot consult with or hire that attorney to represent them, as it creates a conflict of interest for the attorney.*

As you progress through this process and the "you should's…" and "when I got divorced…" conversations with friends or family start, I want to waive that yellow caution flag at you as another reminder:

Don't listen to your friends and family

As the conversation begins, see the yellow caution flag waving in your head and run forest run!! DON'T listen – pretend they are like Charlie Brown talking, and all you can hear is "Wa wa wa wa…." I cannot stress this enough.

While I know they mean well, their advice most often is incorrect and will lead you down the wrong path(s), set you up with unrealistic expectations, and sometimes cause adverse results in your divorce case.

It is not required to retain the services of an attorney to navigate a legal divorce, it is not always necessary, and sometimes it is not the best strategy. The services of an attorney can be retained at any point in time during your case.

You may get started with the process of representing yourself, and you may find you can navigate the entire process without attorney representation, or you may find that you need an attorney at a certain point to help address a particular issue. There are many effective ways to advocate through the process while limiting the expense of attorney services.

In a later Chapter, we will discuss various types of divorce support professionals available, their role, and a general idea of the scope of services they may provide.

As you begin to deal with divorce's legal process, check

your emotions at the door. Here's another reminder that the legal forum is NOT the place to deal with the emotional angst that is inevitably part of the divorce. To advocate effectively in the legal process: it is important to maintain a separation between the feelings and the legal process.

Let's get down to the brass tacks, the legal process of divorce! It may or may not be a surprise to learn that research has shown, characteristically, more women initiate divorce than men; **AND** "...divorced women are typically happier after ending their marriages." (Bagshaw, Joanne, 2017, Psychology Today, Who Initiates Divorce More Often?) I know I am, and you will be too!!

The back of this Guidebook contains completed examples for each family law legal form discussed throughout, that assume the wife is the Petitioner.

The steps for the *Initial Filing, Stage 1,* of the legal process for divorce begins are as follows:

1. Complete the *Initial Filing* forms;
2. File the *Initial Filing* forms with the appropriate Court; and
3. Personal service of the *Initial Filing* forms on the other spouse.

Initial Filing
Required Forms

Summons (FL-110)

Petition – Marriage/Domestic Partnership (FL-100)

If, you and your spouse have minor children from then include:

Declaration Under Uniform Child Custody Jurisdiction and Enforcement Act (FL-105)

The purpose of the *Petition for Dissolution* is to tell the Court that a lawsuit for divorce is being started and placing the issues to be decided, such as property division, custody, support, etc. in the jurisdiction of the Court so that they may make final orders and judgments on the matter.

I have seen so many individuals mistakenly believe that the mere filing of the *Petition for Dissolution* and checking the box indicating "spousal support" or some other issue will result with the Court setting a hearing, that is "Stinkin' Thinkin'," the filing of the *Petition for Dissolution,* WILL NOT, trigger the Court to set a hearing.

If there is a need for Court intervention to obtain Court Orders until a final resolution is reached, then a form known as a "Request for Order (FL-300)" must be filed and served, for you to get a hearing date set with the Court, this form and the process are discussed in detail later in this Guidebook.

Once the **Stage 1 - Initial Filing** required forms have been personally served on the Responding spouse, a *Proof of Service of Summons (FL-115)* must be filed with the Court. It is proof to the Court of: the location, date, and time the Responding Spouse was served with the required forms for the **Initial Filing**. The form also requires, the name and contact information of the person that effectuated service.

> *After Personal Service of required forms for the Initial Filing*
>
> *Prepare and File: Proof of Service of Summons* **(FL-115).**

It is the responsibility of the Petitioner to:

- Arrange for someone, over the age of 18 years of age, that is not a party to this divorce action, to personally deliver (serve) the **Initial Filing** forms, to the responding spouse.
- Make sure that person completes, signs and returns the *Proof of Service of Summons (FL-115)*; and

64

- File the *Proof of Service of Summons (FL-115)* with the Court. An example of the completed *Proof of Service of Summons (FL-115)* is provided at the end of this Guidebook.

Automatic Temporary Restraining Orders "ATROS's"

Read and pay attention to back of the Summons (FL-110).

The back of the Summons (FL-110) has "Automatic Temporary Restraining Orders", commonly referred to as "ATROS's".

These go into full force and effect as soon as the responding spouse is personally served with the Summons (FL-110) and Petition (FL-100).

It is important to read and observe these "ATRO's" as they place certain limitations on the parties .

Responding to the Petition for Dissolution

Once the responding party has received personal service of the required forms for **Stage 1 - Initial Filing**, the legal clock starts, AND decisions must begin to be made.

At this point in **Stage 1**, the **Initial Filing** forms now have been filed and served, and the responding party has 30-days time to file their response to the *Petition for Dissolution (FL-100)*. Whether you are the Petitioner or Respondent, this is a good time to start to gather, organize and prepare the **financial disclosure** forms for **Stage 2**, so they may be finalized and ready for service on the other party, promptly and in the timeframe prescribed by law.

The Respondent has 30 days from the date of personal service to file and serve:

Response– Marriage/Domestic Partnership (FL-120) IF,

there are minor child(ren) of the marriage:

Declaration Under Uniform Child Custody Jurisdiction and Enforcement Act (FL-105)

Not every case will require that the responding party file a *Response to Dissolution (FL-120)*. It is the first fork in the divorce road; whether or not the responding party needs to file a *Response to Dissolution (FL-120)* and pay another filing fee is ultimately determined by how amicable the spouses are, their ability to be reasonable, communicate effectively, and capacity to reach an amicable agreement on all the issues.

To Respond or Not to Respond?

Below is a chart that reflects each scenario for the responding party. As your own advocate, this information is helpful, to ensure the appropriate forms are included in the Stage 3, final Judgment packet, ultimately submitted to the Court for Judge's signature.

Response Options	Resulting Path for Stage 3, Final Judgment
No Response Filed; No Written Agreement. When the Responding Party, for whatever reason, does not participate in the process or engage in settlement negotiations.	*"True Default"* The Judge will base their decision on what is requested in the Petition for Dissolution.
No Response Filed; With a Written Agreement. When the parties work together to reach an amicable agreement.	*"Default"* The responding party has a voice in the outcome; as the parties worked together to reach a written agreement known as a "Marital Settlement Agreement".
Response filed; Written Agreement. The responding party filed and served a Response to Dissolution; however; the parties were able to reach a written agreement.	*"Uncontested"* The responding party has a pony in the race by filing and serving the Response, AND eventually, the parties worked out a written agreement.
Response filed; No Written Agreement. Parties are unable to reach a written Agreement.	*"Contested"* Both parties have a pony in the race; the parties are unable to reach an agreement, and the Court must decide the final outcome.

PART TWO

The Middle

"Avoiding danger is no safer in the long run than outright exposure. The fearful are caught as often as the bold" - **Helen Keller**

CHAPTER EIGHT

STAGE 2 – FINANCIAL DISCLOSURES

"I'm not afraid of storms, for I'm learning how to sail my ship." - **Louisa May Alcott**

Remember those financial documents discussed in an earlier Chapter? Well, have them out organized and ready to move forward to **Stage 2 – the Financial Disclosures**. California law requires that each spouse serve the other spouse, in writing, an itemization of everything owned and owed, by either or both of you, as of the date of separation.

The accurate and timely completion of the preliminary financial disclosure forms is often where delays in the process begin to occur. While California Family Code § 2104 provides for a specific timeframe that each spouse is required to serve the other with their *Preliminary Declaration of Disclosure* information; throughout my lengthy 30-year legal career, it is not uncommon for clients to fail to provide their preliminary financial disclosures promptly, even when an attorney is handling the case.

As a Paralegal, I have found getting clients to timely complete and serve the financial disclosure documents can sometimes feel like pulling teeth. It's so interesting to me because, the purpose of these financial disclosure documents is, so each party has a complete understanding and knowledge of all the stuff everyone is fighting about:

- The Marital assets and debts known to each party as of the date of separation; and
- The income earned by each spouse.

Pursuant to Family Code § 2104, each party serves the other with a Preliminary and a Final Declaration of Disclosure. The parties may waive the *final* Declaration of Disclosure; however, the Preliminary Financial Disclosure forms service is mandatory.

Strategic Tip

Household, furniture, furnishings and appliances are usually assigned a "fire sale" value; if your spouse indicates a value far higher than the actual worth of the item listed; let your spouse be awarded that item at their listed value; and you will receive a credit on your side for half of that "overly valued" item.

The *Financial Disclosure* forms are part of the most critical information in the legal divorce process. To satisfy legal requirements, the Court has created forms containing categories for the information to include in the *financial disclosures* concerning all assets, debts, and income information for each spouse.

This information should provide a financial roadmap of the marital assets and debts that existed as of the date of separation, that eventually will be divided between each spouse. You can use this financial information as you move towards **Stage 3, Final Judgment**, where you and your spouse will begin to negotiate realistic settlement options to reach a final settlement agreement that is fair and equitable for both spouses.

As part of the **financial disclosures**, income information for each spouse must be included as this information is necessary to formulate decisions regarding spousal support and child support, both temporary and long-term, if applicable. For temporary orders for child and/or spousal support, see Chapter on, *Navigating the Courts*.

When preparing to gather this information, I often recommend that my clients get a fresh notepad, pen, video camera and/or camera; go from room to room making notes and photographing furniture, etc., in each room. It is not necessary to list every fork, knife, spoon, or piece of garbage that's in the house unless, of course, it has some sort of intrinsic value.

Look at the financial disclosures, like baking of a pie, if you will:

The financial information and statements = the ingredients.

The values of the marital assets and marital debts = the size (and maybe even the flavor and texture).

Then an assessment can be made = how to slice the pie.

The intent is to have each party receive the same amount of pie.

Maybe the slices are disproportionate in size; but together, all the slices equal ½ the pie, for each spouse.

The Courts have made it fairly simple to meet the **financial disclosure** requirements. The forms make it easy to identify each asset and debt by providing categories, with instructions for the backup documentation necessary to attach as proof.

The Court will not allow a final Judgement to be entered if the parties have failed to file a *Proof of Service of Declaration of Disclosure (FL-141)*. This form confirms to the Court that each spouse has served the required financial disclosures.

Financial Disclosure Forms

Declaration of Disclosure (FL-140)

Attach copies of tax returns filed by you for the past two(2) years.

(This form ***does not*** get filed with the Court.)

Schedule of Assets and Debts (FL-142)

Review the form and attach copies of any required deeds, title, statements, etc.

(This form ***does not*** get filed with the Court.)

Income and Expense Declaration (FL-150)

Attach copies of the last two(2) months' pay stubs, or if self-employed, Schedule C, from your most recent tax return.

(***IF*** there are issues of child support and/or spousal or partner support, then this form ***DOES*** get filed with the Court.)

Declaration Regarding Service of Declaration of Disclosure (FL-141)

(This form ***DOES*** get filed with the Court ***after*** the above forms have been served on the other party.)

Proof of Service by Mail (FL-335*)***, to be completed and signed by the person who mailed the documents, must complete and sign.

Be sure to black out any social security and/or account numbers, leaving only the last 4 digits showing. The ***financial disclosures*** should be complete to the satisfaction of each of the parties before moving forward to **Stage 3** of the divorce process. Make sure you feel comfortable that the **financial disclosure** in **Stage 2** are complete. Which means:

- The preliminary financial disclosures have been completed and served by each spouse.
- Each spouse agrees and is comfortable that all the information is truthfully and accurately disclosed.
- No issues require further information to be received from you or the other spouse that requires the "Discovery" process.

"Discovery" Process

The law provides a legal remedy to help ascertain financial documents, information statements, etc. This process is known as "Discovery." The "Discovery" process is a standard part of the legal process; the legal method used by a person engaged in a lawsuit to gather evidence. The "stuff" received as part of the "Discovery" process may be used as evidence during a court hearing or trial should the need arise.

What is "Discovery"?

The American Bar Association defines it as "...the formal process of exchanging information between the parties about the witnesses and evidence they'll present at trial."

Before we delve more into the "Discovery" process, I want to provide some Paralegal perspective based on my experience as a Paralegal regarding the "Discovery" process. "Discovery" is an essential tool when dealing with a high-conflict spouse. Often, one spouse is the one that has most of the financial information.

The purpose of "Discovery" is to obtain to gather documentation and information necessary for the determination of issues such as:

Division of marital property and debt.

Determination of custody and visitation.

Determination of child support.

Determination of spouse support.

If you know that your spouse has no useful documentation and/or information to contribute, avoid the desire to engage in a *"tit for tat"* strategy by retaliating with unnecessary "Discovery" requests. This pointless tact will only prolong the divorce case, frustrate the legal process, and make attorney fees begin to spiral out of control.

Unnecessary "tit for tat" motivated strategies

As a Paralegal, during the "Discovery" phase, I witnessed the *"tit for tat"* strategy backfire, resulting in large attorney fees and disappointed clients.

"Discovery" can be an important part of the evidentiary legal process, it is also a process that tends to run up excessive, often times, unnecessary attorney fees and cause continued delays in the legal process.

In my professional experience, it is a standard part of the legal practice for an attorney to serve the opposing spouse with Form Interrogatories (FL-145) and Demand for Production and Inspection of Documents (C.C.P. §2031).

There are legal timelines for serving and responding to the various methods of "Discovery"; along with legal ramifications should a party fail, refuse or falsely answer "Discovery" requests. The person responding to the "Discovery" request(s) must sign and verify the accuracy of the response and all documents included; further, the response(s) must be signed under penalty of perjury.

Let's take a look at the terminology associated with various methods of "Discovery":

- The "Propounding Party" is the spouse that is asking for the information.
- The "Responding Party" is the spouse that is responding with the information.
- To help as you advocate for yourself through this process; below is a list of a few of the more commonly used modes of "Discovery," with the related statutory reference for ease of research as you educate yourself on the law, guidelines, and procedures that go with the respective method.

Each spouse is entitled to use the "Discovery" process while engaged in a lawsuit for divorce.

Common modes of "Discovery" used in family law cases:

- **Form Interrogatories (FL-145) - C.C.P. § 2030.030 - This is a pre-approved Judicial**

Counsel form covering each issue involved in the Divorce process from the name, social security number, income information, children, gifts, and more.

In my experience, and based upon what I learned working for attorneys when advocating on your behalf, unless the parties are completely amicable on the issues of money and children, the use of Form Interrogatories (at a minimum) FL-145) is a way to easily confirm information.

- **Demand for Production and Inspection of Documents - C.C.P. § 2031.030**

This Document usually asks you to produce every document, including the kitchen sink. Most of the time, the majority of the documents that are requested probably won't apply. When answering these, it's necessary to provide the documentation you have in your possession; you don't have to run around to the banks and get documents that are hard to get; that is where those subpoenas come in and can be used to get records from banks.

- **Specially Prepared Interrogatories - C.C.P. § 2030.030 and 2030.050**

A series of questions specifically drafted questions prepared by one spouse to be served on the other spouse.

- **Subpoenas duce tecum - C.C.P. § 1987**

This document will force a person, such as a witness, to appear in Court, and bring specific documents when they appear.

- **Requests for Admission of Truth of Facts or Genuineness of Documents -**

C.C.P. § 2033.010

It is a series of questions used to:

  - Establish the truth of specified facts,

  - Admit a legal conclusion,

  - Determine a spouse's opinion relating to a particular fact,

  - Settle an issue in controversy, and

  - Admit the genuineness of specified documents.

- **Depositions - C.C.P. § 2025.010**

A set of questions asked and answered orally and under oath. The responses are recorded by a Court reporter and printed into written form, known as a transcript.

CHAPTER NINE

REQUESTING ORDERS FROM THE COURT

"Don't compromise yourself. You are all you've got."
- **Janis Joplin**

During the divorce process, there may be a need for the Court to make interim or "temporary" orders on issues such as custody, visitation, child support, spousal support, the possible sale of the residence, etc., until **Stage 3, Final Judgment**, is reached. To achieve this: a *Request for Order (FL-300)* can be filed with the Court at any time throughout the divorce process by either party to request the court make or modify "temporary" orders. This form is commonly referred to as "R.F.O."

Don't get confused with the term *"temporary orders."* It simply means that the orders made by the court are "temporary" until further orders of the court are made, a marital settlement agreement is entered into by the parties, or the parties go to trial.

"Final Orders" are the Judgment which will either be reached by way of a Marital Settlement Agreement signed by both parties or Trial wherein the judge will make the final orders because the parties could not reach an agreement.

See Guidebook Stage 3, Final Judgement.

Steps to file a *Request for Order (FL-300)* with the court:

1. Submit "R.F.O." to the court clerk for filing;
2. Court clerk with file and assign a hearing date;
3. The court clerk will return a "conformed copy" to the filing party; and
4. The party will then need to serve a "conformed copy" on the other spouse with a blank *Responsive Declaration (Form FL-320)*.

If the "R.F.O." is filed after the **Stage 1 - Initial Filing** forms have already been served on the responding spouse, then the "R.F.O." may be served by mail and file with the Court:

Proof of Service by Mail (FL-335)

Requesting Orders for Custody/Visitation

If orders for Custody and/or Visitation are being requested, the Court will also set the matter for Child Custody Recommending Counseling (CCRC), and the Court Clerk will issue an Order to Attend Child Custody Recommending Counseling, which will need to be served on your spouse with the "R.F.O."

Both parties attend the CCRC and then the subsequent hearing. At the CCRC, the "Mediator" will make a written recommendation to the court about Custody/Visitation.

Before the court hearing, each of you will have a chance to review the Mediator's recommendation and make notes about any changes you wish to ask the judge to make. At the time of the hearing, you can ask the judge to make any changes and/or modifications, and the judge will let you know whether or not they agree when the ruling is issued.

Requesting Orders for Support

At the start of the divorce, there may be a need for some immediate monetary relief, in the form of spousal and/or child support. Spousal support and child support work differently, and it is important to have a general understanding of how each works, and how to get a "temporary order" in place before reaching a final agreement, specifically if your spouse will not agree to provide some type of interim support voluntarily.

If there is a need for "temporary" support, then a *Request for Order (FL-300)* and a current *Income and Expense Declaration (FL-150)* will need to be properly prepared and filed with the court and served on the other party. The "R.F.O." should include an explanation to the Court as to why there is a need for the orders requested in the "R.F.O." Note, the Court will consider an Income and Expense Declaration (FL-150) as "current" as long as it was filed within 90 days before the hearing date.

Spousal Support

There is quite a bit of "Stinkin' Thinkin'" when it comes to the topic of spousal support. The purpose of spousal support is to provide the lower-earning spouse income to survive while getting back on their feet and becoming self-supporting. The Court does not like to see people solely dependent upon spousal support, even in cases where marriages may be considered as "long-term."

Don't make the mistake of assuming:

- You will get spousal support.
- The amount of spousal support you may receive.

- The length of time you may receive spousal support.
- In situations where one spouse earned significantly more than the other spouse, there may be a need for spousal support. Unlike child support, spousal support is not mandatory and left to the sole discretion of the Court.

Child Support

The state of California wants parents to support their children; therefore, child support must be addressed when there are minor children involved. In cases involving minor children, there is no question that child support needs to be addressed at some point, usually sooner than later. Each state has its child support laws.

Once a parenting plan is established, the custodial timeshare is used as part of the formula to calculate the monthly child support obligation. In my experience as a Paralegal, clients are always cautioned when referencing child custody and visitation, **DO NOT speak in terms of percentages**. For instance, don't go into a custody mediation and say to them, "I want 50/50 custody."

First, the joint legal and joint physical is not the same as a 50/50 timeshare. We will get into those definitions and parenting schedules in the *Custody & Timeshare* Chapter . To help advocate the proper child support amounts, you can get a general idea of likely child support calculations by visiting online the *Department of Child Support Services* website, where you will find a child support calculator. There you can plug in the appropriate income, timeshare, and any applicable information requested for the calculation; it will then generate the guideline child support along with possible temporary spousal support amounts.

At the time of the hearing, the Judge will only make Orders with reference to the issues included in the "R.F.O." that is set to be heard on that date and time. Remember that just because your spouse has requested something in their "R.F.O." does not mean the judge will grant it. A spouse may "request" whatever it is they desire in their "R.F.O."

This is the way to tell the court and the opposing party of their desired outcome for the hearing.

CHAPTER TEN

CUSTODY AND TIMESHARE SCHEDULES

"Children have never been very good at listening to their elders," but they've never failed to imitate them." - **James Baldwin, novelist, and social critic**

Society has created this stigma that we somehow fail our children if we do not stay married. As a mother, I know the safety and well-being of our kids are always our priority and biggest concern. In my personal and professional experience, I have seen far more damage caused to children living in a toxic environment than has ever been caused by the need to move between 2 homes.

If you have been married to a high-conflict spouse and living in a toxic environment, if you think your kids are unaware of it or unaffected by it, you're **WRONG**! "Staying for the sake of the children" is a major mistake for the health and well-being of you and your children. The children live in the toxic energy that fills the house; they hear the yelling, see the arguing, and feel the tension!!

Kids are far more resilient than we realize or get credit for, the adults are not quite as resilient. Adults tend to have a more narrow-minded scope of view than children often do.

Children are also way more astute than you may realize. If you think you have been hiding the fighting, unhappiness, or whatever it is that has gone on in your home, you're not. The child(ren) probably is aware of far more than you realize. They are collateral damage in the "war" between you and your spouse. Obviously, the more amicable the 2 spouses can be, the better off everyone will be, including the child(ren).

You will see, once the high-conflict spouse is no longer around to cause chaos and disruption, you and your children will begin to thrive in the new peaceful surroundings and positive environment you will be able to create.

- Keep an open line of communication with your child(ren).
- Allow them to vent and be upset.
- Don't put down or make disparaging remarks about your ex-spouse.
- Don't allow a third party to make disparaging remarks about the other parent in front of the child(ren).
- Don't expect the children to share your viewpoint about the other parent.
- Don't discuss the divorce case with or in front of the children.
- Don't use the children as messengers to make schedule changes.
- Don't use the child(ren) as part of a strategic plan.
- Seek counseling to help the child(ren) acclimate to these life changes.
- Make sure the child(ren) understands this is not their

fault.

- Allow the children access to both parents.
- Don't expect the child(ren) to be your support system.
- The child(ren) doesn't need to know about your financial circumstances.
- The child(ren) don't need to know about your anger towards your spouse.
- The child(ren) doesn't need to know any transgressions that may have occurred by you or your spouse.

~ Keep in Mind ~

*That A$$ H*** is still the other parent of your child(ren).*

Co-parenting with a high-conflict spouse is difficult, if not impossible, and may require Court intervention, depending on the circumstances. It is important to always remain on the high road talked about earlier in this Guidebook. Always encourage the child(ren) to go when it is the other parent's timeshare, even if the child(ren) is reluctant to go. Unless, of course, there are issues of domestic violence, sexual abuse, or you feel there is some danger, then, of course, seek the authorities and professional guidance immediately.

Parenting Plans

People misunderstand the terminology connected with custody, visitation, timeshare, and parenting plans all the time. Let's fix that so as you advocate for yourself; you don't make that same mistake.

Physical custody refers to where the child is physically in the care of the parent.

Legal custody refers to the party with authority to decide for that child about education, medical, healthcare, and religion.

Joint legal and **joint physical** custody refers to both parents having a significant amount of time with the minor child(ren), physically and both parents also have a say in the child(ren)'s medical care, education, religion.

Creating a Parenting Plan.

When there is a minor child(ren) involved, the 1st priority is to create and agree on an effective parenting plan that meets the child's needs. It can get a bit tricky and contentious at times, especially in situations that involve a high-conflict spouse.

In cases involving a high-conflict spouse, it's important to develop a safe and effective mode of communication for purposes of sharing co-parenting information. The Courts have online communication programs called, Our Family Wizard or Talkingparents.org, which allow the Court to monitor the conversations between both of you.

When considering an effective parenting plan, always be sure; it is in the best interest of the child(ren). Below are some suggestions to consider factoring in:

- The child(ren)'s school, social and extracurricular activities.
- The schedules for each parent.
- The ages of the child(ren).
- The different needs of children at different ages.
- A baby needs much more care and time and attention than a teenager with friends and activities and places to go and things to do and people to see.
- Be fair to the children while also ensuring that they get quality time with both parents.
- Your work schedule.

- Your spouse's work schedule.
- Your child(ren)'s activity schedule.
- Your child(ren)'s school schedule.
- The needs of the children.
- The safety, health, and welfare of the children.
- The lifestyle of each spouse.

The co-parenting schedule should include holidays, vacation time from school, and weekends. Sometimes there is a need for a little flexibility when it comes to requests for changes in scheduling; this can be done on an as-need basis, keeping in mind, what's good for the goose is good for the gander.

Except for cases involving domestic violence, the majority of parents share joint legal, joint physical custodial arrangements with various timeshares schedules based upon what works in the best interest of the children, the needs of the children, the safety, health, and welfare of the children and the family lifestyle.

As a tool to aid as you advocate through **Stage 2** of the process, the next page contains a chart demonstrating the timeshare percentage to calculate child support.

A few common timeshare plans.

- 50-50 timeshare. It is an equal timeshare plan between the parents, many times; this results in a week on/week off timeshare between them.
- 2-3 timeshare plan. This timeshare plan has the child(ren) spend two(2) days with Parent 1 and 2, two days with Parent 2, and then back three(3) And then the next week they switch, so on and so forth.
- 2-2-5-5 timeshare plan. This timeshare plan has a minor child(ren) 2 days with each parent and five (5)

days with the other parent. And then there the minor child(ren) alternate weeks for one parent, the child(ren)'s with one parent one week, and then the next week with the other parent. And then that goes back and forth every week they change.

- 2-week schedule. This timeshare has the minor child(ren) spend two(2) weeks with one parent and then goes back and spends 2 weeks with the other parent.

- 3-4-4-3 Timeshare. This timeshare has the minor child(ren) spend three(2) days with one parent, four(4) days with the other; then it switches. The minor child(ren) spends four(4) days with the first parent and then three(3) days.

- Alternating, every 2-day timeshare. This timeshare has the child(ren) switch between parents every two(2) days.

There are many ways to create a timeshare that works for the circumstances of your family dynamic. It is meant to provide an idea of some common timeshare schedules. Then as an advocate, you must assess your life and decide what the least disruptive for the child(ren) and the 2 of you as parents is. Some schedules work better for younger children, while others work better for older children.

2 weekends per month	13%
1 weekend per month and 1 evening per week	14%
Alternate weekends	14%
Alternate weekends + 2 summer weeks	18%
Alternate weekends, ½ holidays, and 2 summer weeks	19%
Alternate weekends, ½ holidays and 2 summer weeks - Parent 2 also has 2 summer weeks -	18%
Two 3-day weekends per month	20%
Two 2½-day weekends per month	16%
Alternate weekends and 1 evening per week	21%
Alternate weekends and 1 overnight per week	28%
Alternate 3-day weekends	21%
Alternate 2½-day weekends	18%
Alternate weekends, ½ holidays and 4 summer weeks - alternate summer weekends with makeups -	21%
Alternate weekends, ½ holidays, and 4 summer weeks -no alternating summer weekends-	21%
Alternate weekends & ½ holidays and ½ summer -with or without alternate summer weekends-	22%
Alternate 3-day weekends plus 1 evening per week	28%
Alternate 2½-day weekends plus 1 evening per week	25%
Alternate 3-day weekends plus 1 overnight Weekend per week	36%
Alternate 2½-day weekends plus 1 overnight weekend per week	32%

Alternate Weekend, 1/2 Holidays, 1 Evening/Week, 4 Summer Weeks -alternate weekends in summer, with makeups-	28%
Alternate Weekends, 1 Evening/Week When School is in Session, and 1/2 School Vacation	28%
3 days per week	43%
First, third, and fifth weekends	15%
First, third, fifth, 3-day weekends	23%
First, third, fifth, 2½-day weekends	19%
First, third, and alternate fifth weekends	14%
First, third, alternate fifth 3-day weekends	21%
First, third, alternate fifth 2½-day weekends	18%

Now that we've established some possible parenting plan options, how does that get put into place?

- Agreement between the parties; or
- Court order.

If the 2 of you can immediately agree upon a custody/timeshare plan that works for everybody, that's the best-case scenario. However, if you can't and Court intervention is required, then a *Request for Order (FL-300)* can be filed with the Court. Often, the Court's parenting plan will end up as part of the final marital settlement agreement; if the parties find the schedule is working for them and the child(ren).

Parenting Through the Process

If you and your spouse are amicable, then a less formal interim parenting plan can be put in place while working towards *Stage 3, Final Judgment*. When dealing with a high-conflict spouse, it may be necessary to file a *Request for Order (FL-300)* and ask the Court to issue temporary custody, visitation, and child support orders.

Parenting through a divorce can be complicated, which is why it is important to get some form of a temporary parenting plan in place as soon as possible. It will help avoid conflict, misunderstandings and ensure the children have scheduled access to both parents.

Remember that high road, do your part by providing the other parent's contact information to the school or any necessary third-party. To ensure your spouse receives the same information about the child(ren) as you. Any information you receive through coaches, schools, teachers, or any educators or professional authority involved in your children's life; should be shared with the other parent.

Co-parenting with a high-conflict spouse is exhausting and frustrating. If you are dealing with a high-conflict spouse and a conflict or situation should occur, make sure to document each incident on a calendar to recall the date and details. Use a calendar to log the date, time, and details of the "bad behavior" demonstrated by the other parent. When the time comes, this will make it easier to recount and demonstrate this information to the Court.

If there are issues with the other parent's lack of responsibility when meeting their custodial and/or timeshare obligations, note those dates and times when the other parent is late, either picking up or dropping off the child(ren) on your calendar as well.

Acting as your advocate, documenting these things will help you demonstrate a behavior pattern should the need arise.

The online communication apps, talkingparents.org and

myfamilywizard.com, can be viewed and monitored by the Court; this helps eliminate the need for contact between the parents. Research has shown that eliminating the communication between high-conflict couples reduces anger and hostility over time.

In situations involving a high conflict spouse, you may need to find alternative means for communication regarding the children, such as:

- A court-monitored program: talking parents of Our Family Wizard.
- Email.
- Some form of online communication.
- Avoid aggressive communications between the 2 of you.

At the end of the day, remember the kids are watching you; the happiness, safety, and well-being are of first and foremost importance.

CHAPTER ELEVEN

EMERGENCY HEARINGS

"If we can limit the unproductive interactions, we will be able to better focus on productive ones."

— Rachel G. Scott

A need may arise where you feel there is a situation that requires immediate Court intervention. It is what is referred to as an Ex Parte hearing. Check your local court for the rules and procedures before proceeding, as there are very specific rules and procedures that must be followed to be successful with filing the documents.

Once you submit an Ex Parte "RFO" to the Court with all the necessary information and evidence regarding the issue at hand; the court will then determine if there are difficult circumstances that warrant an immediate hearing; if it is denied; it will still be set for hearing just on a later date by the court's regular calendar availability.

Your spouse will need to receive notice, so it is important to check the rules regarding timing and procedure when using this option.

CHAPTER TWELVE

WHAT TO EXPECT WHEN YOU GET TO COURT

"Don't be afraid. Be focused. Be determined. Be hopeful. Be empowered." -

Michelle Obama.

Too often, people mistakenly believe that Court is the magic answer to a conflict with their spouse. They believe they're going to get to court and "tell the judge...", and somehow everything will come out as they expect and are convinced the judge will see it their way ~ WRONG!! "Stinkin' Thinkin'" There is a good chance the Judge's ruling may not be what is envisioned, if at all.

The Judge may not see things the same way as you; in fact, they probably won't see things the same as you at all. In short, before a hearing, the Judge will hopefully have reviewed any documents and evidence filed by both sides; then, at the hearing or trial, each spouse has an opportunity to present their position and/or evidence, then the Judge will issue their ruling. Obviously, this is the short 'n sweet version of what can sometimes feel like an extremely long process.

There are rules, procedures, and any number of things that may occur between the time an "RFO" is filed and the time the Court may render Orders. Be sure to check the local courthouse for rules, procedures, and any possible additional forms that may be required.

Once you open an issue for the Court's decision, the pendulum may swing in either direction. Be sure to do your homework first before filing anything with the Court. I have seen client's blindly file "RFO"'s with the Court, then call me when it backfired on them because they failed to do their research and properly advocate for themselves. Undoing is

FAR harder than doing. It is not easy to undo a Court order, and many times it can be impossible.

Family court is part of our legal justice system; therefore, each side is entitled to due process under our United States Constitution. When anything is filed with the Court, it must be served on the other spouse; they have an opportunity to review what has been filed and respond to the same.

Just because you or your spouse asks for an order from the Court does not mean it will be granted. As an advocate, be sure to do your research before you file or respond to any Court documents.

When dealing with the Court, remain on that "high road" and be prepared with your "Teflon suit" that I recommended. Too often, clients get caught up in the emotions and forget to focus on the real objective. As you proceed toward the Court hearing, parties will exchange Declarations and/or documents related to the issue(s) at hand. Don't be surprised when you read your spouse's statements and their perspective on a situation is in polar opposition to yours or just completely way out in the left field. Stay focused on the issue(s) at hand and your desired result, *nothing more, nothing less*! Remember, wear your business hat; you are acting as an advocate for yourself, so you always need to be sure to have your best foot forward.

DO NOT focus on trying to prove that your spouse is a liar or a jerk. The Court only deals in facts and evidence. I have frequently heard Family Court referred to as "liar's court." The "He's a liar!", "She's a liar!" strategy doesn't work and will get you nowhere fast, even if you know your spouse isn't telling the truth. The reality is that your definition of **fair** may not be what matters or what the judge hears or wants to hear. There will only be a very limited time to get your point and your argument across. That's why it's so important to make sure that you get your story succinct and to the point in the Declaration, you file with your *Request for Order (FL-300)*.

If at all possible, it's always better to try and keep issues amongst the two of you and resolve them yourself; this way, you retain control over the outcome, rather than placing decisions about your life in the hands of a stranger, a Judge, who knows nothing about you or your family, other than what he read in the papers filed by you and your spouse.

At the end of the day, the Judge is a human being, no different than you or I. They may be having a bad day or see things from the same viewpoint as you.

CHAPTER THIRTEEN

DIVORCE SUPPORT PROFESSIONALS

"You can't be what you can't see." - **Mary Wright, Edelman, founder, and president of the children's defense fund**

In this chapter, we'll discuss the various divorce support professionals and their role in the divorce world, how they may help with your divorce and how, in some cases, you can use them instead of a lawyer, particularly when you want to save money.

It's no secret that hiring an attorney can be expensive. You may not know that you can successfully advocate through the legal process without ever hiring an attorney. In cases involving a high-conflict spouse, there may be a necessity to seek legal counsel regarding intervention to protect the safety of yourself and your children if you have them.

Attorney/Lawyer

There is a common misconception about the role of an

attorney and how to utilize their services in the divorce process properly should the need arise. This information can help keep legal fees way down right off the bat. Like the Judge, an Attorney is also human; they are not miracle workers, clairvoyants, or magicians. They have no way to see into the future any more than any of us.

As a paralegal, the complaints I hear from people about their Attorney never cease to amaze me. Many individuals become shocked and disappointed with their family law attorney when they realize they have spent thousands of dollars to learn that the attorney's capacity in the divorce process is limited to the legal arena.

If you retain the services of an attorney, make sure you understand the attorney retainer agreement and how attorney billable hours work so, you don't end up with an enormous bill for simple questions.

It's "Stinkin' Thinkin'" to assume an attorney is the magic fix to all things divorce. Don't make the same costly mistake as so many by hiring an attorney and think they will fix the problems and make everything go away. An Attorney does not have the authority to force anyone to do anything; only the Judge has that authority. Attorneys are not wizards and have no special powers to make things happen magically, or people change. My dad summed it up best in a conversation with me, "Attorney's are advocates that apply the law; they are not problem solvers." Barry D. Silbermann, Esq.

Paralegal

What is a paralegal? How is a paralegal different from an attorney? What does a paralegal typically handle that an attorney does not?

The American Bar Association defines a paralegal as "a legal support professional qualified by education, training, or work experience, who performs substantive legal work that an attorney is responsible for." Paralegals are the primary point of contact for all files assigned. The paralegal actively works on the file, drafts and files, the legal forms, pleadings and motions, and reviews, discovery, strategizes the course of action, provides legal research, enters into settlement negotiations with the opposing attorneys and opposing parties, all under the responsibility of an attorney.

The Paralegal briefs and prepares the attorney(s) for court proceedings. Often the paralegal's role is similar to a Divorce Coach. Their job is dealing with the clients and the emotions that go along with the family law process.

The biggest difference between an attorney and a paralegal is education, licensing and obviously, pay. Of course, an attorney has a Jurist Doctrine and has passed a Bar Exam, and a paralegal has not. The lawyer owes more than the paralegal in student loans, too 😊

Believe it or not, attorneys typically are not familiar with how to complete legal forms, court procedures, or deadlines. Most of the time, they have Paralegal or secretarial support to generate the work and get it out the door.

The paralegal generally becomes the liaison between the client and the Attorney. The paralegal is the person that does the paperwork; the attorney applies the law and appears in Court on your behalf. The paralegal's responsibility is to ensure your case, you, and the attorney all remain on track and meet the required legal deadlines.

All work done by a Paralegal is under the supervision of an attorney, who is ultimately responsible for all work performed by the Paralegal. In family law, attorneys rely heavily on their paralegals to deal with complex legal issues, handle and maintain client and case files. Paralegals are held to a high caliber of standards and expectations regarding experience, skills, and knowledge of both the legal process and the court system.

A good analogy for the role of a Paralegal would be that of the medical profession. In medicine, you're dealing with a nurse or nurse practitioner; the doctor comes in with the official diagnosis, then leaves again. He's busy, his bedside manner is a bit gruff, and no one can afford him, right?

Essentially paralegals are the nurse practitioners of the legal field. Characteristically, a paralegal will have some type of legal education or training. They will have attended 2 to 4 years of college and typically have a bachelor's degree and have attended some type of paralegal program for certification.

The obvious answer is it takes strict knowledge of the law, legal procedures, legal writing, research, and the ability to work in a fast-paced environment. As a long-time Paralegal, I believe it also requires compassion, understanding, and empathy. Often, clients need emotional support, guidance, and understanding more so than legal advice.

Legal Document Assistant

A Legal Document Assistant ("LDA") has a Paralegal education and background many times with law office experience. There is no attorney supervision in this role. An "LDA" is required to register with the County where they perform business. There are standard educational and experience requirements that must be met, and they must carry a bond for $25,000. Legal Document Assistants can help clients easily and efficiently complete, file, track and serve legal documents, and educate their clients about the procedure.

A Legal Document Assistant ("L.D.A.") is far more accessible and affordable than an attorney. They're skilled and experienced in legal procedure, just in a different capacity than hiring an attorney for representation. The Court is very, very particular about the following procedure. They will return incorrect documents causing missed deadlines, etc. It is almost much harder and costly to undo a mistake.

It is cost-effective to pay an experienced divorce professional, such as a Legal Document Assistant, to properly prepare and process the legal paperwork. The rates for an "LDA" will be significantly less than that of an attorney, and you can be assured the paperwork will be properly completed, timely filed, and properly arranged for service by the other party.

As non-attorney, they are not allowed to provide legal advice.

Divorce Coach

A Divorce Coach understands the dynamics involved with high-conflict divorce and can help mediate between you and your spouse, assist in keeping legal fees down, gather the necessary paperwork, help you be prepared, and work with you to develop an action.

The American Bar Association recognizes the role of a Divorce Coach. It is defined as "…a flexible goal-oriented process, designed to support, motivate, and guide people through divorce, to help them make the best possible decisions for their future. Based on their particular interests, needs, and concerns. Divorce Coaches have different professional backgrounds and are selected based on their specific needs for the clients. For example, some divorce coaches are financial planners, mental health professionals, lawyers, or mediators who have experienced divorce, divorcing clients, and ending quotes. They're also paralegals and certified divorce, financial analysts, people who have been through divorce and come from another professional background have gotten an education in the emotional side of divorce.

Certified Divorce Financial Analyst

A Certified Divorce Financial Analyst or CDFA is essentially like a CPA for divorce. According to the Institute for Divorce, their role as a Divorce Professional is to assist clients and their lawyers in understanding how financial decisions may impact the client's financial future. It's important to understand the money, and how money works to make a sound financial decision when reaching a settlement agreement.

Collaborative Law

In the area of family law, people are using various forms of collaborative law, such as mediation, where the parties meet together in a non-litigious environment to reach an amicable agreement between them. Collaborative law is a new way to help spouses try and resolve disputes by removing the litigious faction of it, where everybody works together and sits in a room and tries to come up with a solution that works for everybody, your mediator, your lawyer, your divorce coach, your CDFA, any one of these divorce support professionals can help in the collaborative law process.

Licensed Marriage and Family Therapist (LMFT)

The American Association for Marriage and Family Therapy defines Marriage and Family Therapists (MFTs) as "… mental health professionals trained in psychotherapy and family systems, and licensed to diagnose and treat mental and emotional disorders within the context of marriage, couples and family systems."

The LMFT can be very helpful for both you and your children in helping to deal with the emotional aspects of the divorce process. I went to an LMFT for several months during the beginning of my divorce, and I found it extremely helpful to gain clarity as I began to move forward in the process.

PART THREE

The New Beginning Growing From We To Me™

"If we can limit the unproductive interactions, we will be able to better focus on productive ones." — **Rachel G. Scott**

CHAPTER FOURTEEN

STAGE 3- FINAL JUDGMENT - SETTLEMENT AGREEMENT OR TRIAL

"Accept responsibility for your life. Know that it is you who will get you where you want to go. No one else." **- Les Brown**

So close, yet so far, the bumpy road hasn't ended just yet. When a decision has been made to separate, individuals will frequently begin formulating settlement options in an unwitting attempt to jump right to a **Stage 3, final Judgment**. The reasons stated by my clients vary; nevertheless, the underlying motivation to jump to the end of the process is generally they "just want to be done." You have probably had those same feelings and/or thoughts along this divorce journey.

Trying to rush through the process is understandable; nevertheless, it is not wise. To avoid disputes along the way, keep a written log should either of you decide to divide up household furniture, furnishings, personal belongings, or any other asset along the way.

Stage 3, final Judgment, is when it becomes essential to:

- Wear your advocacy business hat.

- Check those personal emotions at the door.

- Have a clear and concise understanding of **Stage 2, financial disclosures.**

- Avoid basing anything on a "verbal" agreement; get everything in writing.

- Be realistic and open to discuss possible options.

- Have clarity and understanding of both short and long-term financial impact.

- Consider future needs and wants.

- Hide your buttons.

- Use strong negotiation tactics.

- Advocate for yourself!

Tips	
Don't negotiate against yourself.	Send a letter of strong, reasonable settlement proposal with an expiration date for the offer.
Don't "back in" to an argument.	Use overstated Values to your benefit
Use understated Values to your benefits.	Don't be unreasonable.

Nothing is final until the *Judgement (FL-180)* is signed by a Judge and filed by the Court! The best strategy before making any final transfers of real or personal property, if possible, is to wait until **after** each of you sign the settlement AND the *Judgement (FL- 180)* has been entered by the Court.

It's almost a given that the road to **Stage 3, final Judgment**, may be bumpy, with unexpected twists and turns along the way. Some worse than others, dependent upon the type of spouse you are dealing with, amicable or high-conflict. As you advocate through the final stage of the divorce process, congratulations, you join the ranks of "Over 4.3 million court users..." that have also navigated this process without attorney representation, which means you can do it too!!

You should now comprehend the reason, **Stage 2, financial disclosures**, are such a vital part of this process. It is when you take this information and begin to strategize a settlement proposal. Draft a letter and submit it to your spouse as an attempt to settle your matter. To keep things moving along, provide a deadline for responding to the offer; if no response is received, the offer will expire.

Tip

Getting and order and collecting on order are 2 very different things!!

When thinking about a settlement plan; keep in mind the idiom "Bird in hand is worth 2 in the bush." It is best to avoid agreements that leave you to chase down the money from your spouse later down the line.

The reality is, this is a life-changing event; you are both humans with complex feelings and emotions that have an obvious breakdown in communication; trying to work out a "business agreement"; while dealing with the inevitable fallout that comes from the "death" of the marriage is difficult no matter the situation.

Review the possible options for settlement based on your desired outcome. Remember the pie analogy, the **Preliminary Financial Disclosures**, should now provide a picture of the "whole pie" that needs to be equally divided between each of you. To effectively advocate the best settlement for yourself, be sure to have a clear understanding of the financial impact of each possibility. Before signing the final agreement, you may want to consult with an attorney or financial profession-nals, such as a CDFA, CPA, or another type of financial professional, to be sure you are receiving your equitable share of the marital estate.

How does property division work? Well, a couch can't be cut in half, so instead of looking at dividing each "piece," look at the total value of what you are receiving and the total value of what the other party is receiving.

The bottom-line **total** value for each of you should be equal. If one party is receiving more than the other, then a determination needs to be made about where to take the funds required to equalize the party with the smaller distribution.

The simple truth is, most of us don't have a big pot of cash sitting around, so any "equalization" payment is generally paid from 1 of 2 sources:

- Proceeds from the sale of the marital residence; or
- One or the other person's retirement account.

When calculating the "equalization" payment, be sure that the equalization amount owed is deducted from the spouse receiving the higher distribution and not the side that is owed the money.

Now it's time to start formulating a settlement proposal and negotiate that final settlement, using the values and amounts from the **financial disclosures** exchanged in **Stage 2**.

If you have trouble communicating with your spouse to reach a final settlement or feel you may be pressed and want support, divorce support professionals (see Chapter Thirteen) can help, mediate, a settlement negotiation that is amicable for both spouses. This approach may help avoid being pressured into agreeing to something you may regret later down the line.

It may be prudent to consult with a financial professional when looking to use a retirement plan as part of an equalization payment; it is vital to comprehend the various valuation method options and the potential resulting values. Customarily, an actuary service is used to help determine the present and future value for retirement.

When formulating a settlement proposal, there are some important factors to keep in mind. For most of us, the bulk of the marital assets are most often comprised of the house and/or possible retirement accounts.

On a spreadsheet or piece of paper, start by creating 2 columns, 1 for you and 1for your spouse, list the value of every item you're getting in your column and put the value of every item your spouse is getting in the respective column; once all assets and debts have been allocated, then total both columns if they are not equal the party with the greater balance owes the party with a lower balance an equalization payment to make the 2 parties equal unless they agree otherwise.

It can sometimes get a little tricky, you have to look to those liquid assets to determine how to equalize both people. Usually, there is not a lot of liquidity or cash laying around; the furniture isn't worth very much, and you can't split the property into pieces.

Once the 2 of you reach a final settlement agreement, before you sign anything:

- Read through the entire Marital Settlement Agreement.
- Understand all the terms and conditions and that it's what you intended.
- Be sure you each can meet all the terms and conditions.
- Confirm the terms are your intended understanding.

Remember there's no going back once a Marital Settlement Agreement ("MSA") has been signed, and the Court enters the *Judgment (FL-180)*; it's a done deal.

Below is a list to provide a general idea of the options available as you make the final trek towards the navigate through, **Stage 3**, to final Judgment for Dissolution (FL- 180):

1. The use of Collaborative Divorce Support Professionals to help mediate and facilitate the reaching of an amicable settlement agreement between both of you.

2. Work together directly with your spouse to reach an amicable settlement agreement between both of you.

3. Lawyer Up – One or the other of you retains the services of a lawyer to navigate the legal process, and either help facilitate an agreement or prosecute the case.

4. One spouse is either "in the wind," they are either unable to be located or are just completely disengaged in the entire process; there is no Response filed and no agreement; the Court must pass Judgment on all the issues.

Remember, nothing is set in stone yet. Nothing is done until the two of you sign your Marital Settlement Agreement and the judge signs the final Judgment. There are only 2 ways of obtaining the final *Judgment for Dissolution* (FL-180), which are:

1. Agreement between the parties; or
2. The Trial, which means, ultimately, a Judge makes the decisions.

Don't forget; you are still traveling along the high road, wearing a sexy Teflon suit. You own this road because you paved it, this is the road to your brighter future, and you did it. You are the writer of your own story and the future story for your children if any.

Chances are, at some point, an agreement will be reached. Once that's done, a Marital Settlement Agreement will be signed by each of you, and the Judgment packet is submitted to the Court.

Whichever road your case may take to **Stage 3, Final Judgment**, it will fall under one of the following categories:

Default with Agreement. When **both sides agree** on all issues. **No response to the petition is filed** with the court because the parties enter into a Marital Settlement Agreement on all issues.

Default with NO Agreement. When the other party is completely non- participatory in the process, **no response to the petition is filed. The court must pass judgment on the divorce issues** because the other spouse has failed to respond or sign the Marital Settlement Agreement.

- **Uncontested**. When a **response IS filed;** or the Respondent has made a general appearance in Court at some point in the case; the parties have trouble

Working towards an agreement, however, eventually, a Marital Settlement Agreement is signed by the parties.

Contested. The parties cannot reach an agreement; a Trial date is set, and at the Trial, each party goes forward with their case, and the Judge ultimately makes the final decision on all issues the parties are unable to agree upon.

State court statistics show, the majority of contested cases ultimately end up with some agreement. Remember, those statistics, less than 1% of cases actually go to trial.

Final Judgment "packet" forms:

*"I'm not afraid of storms, for I'm learning how to sail my ship." - **Louisa May Alcott***

Always be sure to check your local Court's website for the required forms and instructions for filling out and filing. Acting as your advocate, you want to familiarize yourself with as much information about the forms and procedures necessary to navigate the legal divorce process. Once the 2 of you have reached a written agreement, arrangements should be made for each of you to sign the "M.S.A." in front of a Notary Public. Yay!! You've got this – you're almost to the finish line!

It should be no surprise by now; the Court has required forms that need to be submitted with the signed and notarized "M.S.A." Since you checked the website as instructed in earlier Chapters, you should be somewhat familiar with the final forms. Just in case, in this Chapter is a list of the common court forms that are submitted to the Court with the "M.S.A." so that you can receive a final Judgment and complete **Stage 3.**

It is not legal advice and should not be used as such; the purpose is to familiarize individuals advocating on their behalf with forms and information that may be used to complete the legal divorce process.

Judgment Forms	Default NO Agreement	Default with Agreement	Uncontested	Contested
Request to Enter Default (FL- 165)	X	X		
Declaration for Default or Uncontested Dissolution or Legal Separation (FL-170)	X	X	X	
Judgment (FL-180)	X	X	X	X
Marital Settlement Agreement (MSA)		X	X	
Property Declarations (FL-160)	X			
Notice of Entry of Judgment (FL-190)	X	X	X	
Appearance, Stipulations, and Waivers (FL-130)			X	
Stipulation and Waiver of Final Declaration of Disclosure (FL- 144)		X	X	
Property Declarations (FL-160)	X			
Available Attachments:	Custody	Support		
Child Custody and Visitation Order Attachment (FL-341)	X			
Children's Holiday Schedule Attachment (FL-341(C))	X			
Joint Legal Custody Attachment (FL-341E))	X			
*Child Support Information and Order Attachment (FL-342)		X		
Notice of Rights and Responsibilities (FL-192)	X	X		
*Spousal Support Attachment (FL-157)		X		

*FL-150 Income and Expense Declaration (Note - Only 1 I&E needs to be submitted with Judgment if there are issues of both child and spousal support)

Remember the *Proof of Service of Summons (FL-115),* from **Stage 1**, and the *Declaration Regarding Service of Declaration of Disclosure (FL-141),* from **Stage 2**; if they have not yet been filed with the Court, they will need to be submitted to the Court with the *Judgement (FL-180)* and the required ancillary forms in, **Stage 3, Final Judgment**.

As you navigate through **Stage 3**, the final stage of the legal process, and the road gets a bit bumpy, remember the statistics, "...*less than 1% of cases go to trial over all issues.*" (Pro Se Statistics). Advocating on your behalf, even working with a non- lawyer Divorce Support Professional, to successfully navigate the legal process, can save over $27,000 in attorney fees, and have you joining the ranks of over 4.3 million court users that are self-represented in California.

Congratulations! Great job. Be proud of yourself; your brighter future is already underway.

CHAPTER FIFTEEN

GOING FROM WE TO ME™

"Each of us must confront our fears and come face to face with them. How we handle our fears will determine where we go with the rest of our lives. To experience adventure or to be limited by the fear of it." - **Judy Blume**

You've built a life and a relationship with another person, and now that they are each ended, there can be a tremendous amount of uncertainty and pressure to make the right decisions to protect your well-being and livelihood.

Hope for the best and prepare for the worst. That's what I always do. Focus on what's real, be real with yourself, and set realistic expectations for the outcome. Have your feet grounded in reality. You've got this!!

Golden Rules

Don't have unrealistic expectations.

Surround yourself with the appropriate support team.

Check emotions at the door.

While going through this process, one of the most important things to remember is **_YOU_** and the amazing future you get to create. Don't laser focus on the divorce; focus on the future and the positive. It's very easy to get so lost dealing with the divorce process and overwhelming yourselves with all these details of life that we lose ourselves. Make sure to take time to decompress and take care of yourself throughout this process.

The most important thing to do is sometimes just STOP thinking about everything and turn it all off:

- The divorce
- The kids
- The money
- The house
- Blah blah blah, the list goes on and on.

It's important to take the time and disconnect from all of it; read a good book, watch a movie, take a hot bath, go for a walk, go to the gym, paint, redecorate, listen to music. It doesn't matter what it is, find something that feels good to you, makes you happy, and that belongs to only you. It will help you heal and grow inside.

I always loved to travel; I also had the desire to further my education and start a business; once my ex was out of my life. **_I did it all and more_**!! I went back to college, earned my BA in Business Administration, took a course to earn a TESOL Certification to teach English overseas. I traveled to Thailand for three months and did just that, I taught English to Korean kids. Of course, my daughter was off in college at this point. Obviously, your "me" time will need to be tailor to fit your lifestyle. If there are small children, it's not quite as easy to take off to Thailand. Although, it can be done, just sayin'.

Don't look at this as a negative time. See it as a positive time. It's a rebirth. It's your rebirth. When you *grow* **From We to Me**™, you emerge from the divorce process a whole new person. You will feel empow*HER*ed, resilient, and be an independent individual.

You can be whoever you want to be; however you want to be, whenever you want to be, wherever you want to be, the choice is yours, and the possibilities are endless!

Someone recently shared a story that resonated with me; the analogy demonstrates the perspectives of individuals when faced with adversity in their life.

When a **carrot**, **egg,** and **coffee** are all placed in boiling water, they each react differently.

The Carrot:

Started hard, tough and relentless. When submerged into boiling water, the **carrot**

got soft, weak, and mushy.

The Egg:

Started a delicate, liquid center held in by a thin outer shell. When submerged into boiling water, the insides of the **egg** become hard.

The Coffee:

Started as a unique bean with a hard shell. When submerged into boiling water,

coffee changed the water to a delicious drink.

Which one do you want to be when you *grow* **From We to Me**™, the **Carrott,** the **Egg**, or the **Coffee?**

INSTRUCTIONS AND CHECKLISTS

"Freeing yourself was one thing, claiming ownership of that freed self was another." – **Toni Morrison**

Stage 1 – Initial Case Forms

<u>Petitioner</u>

Step 1: Prepare forms to start a Divorce case.

Summons (FL-110)

Petition – Marriage/Domestic Partnership (FL-100)

Declaration of Residence (RI-FL-036)

IF there is a minor child(ren) of the marriage:

Declaration Under Uniform Child Custody Jurisdiction and Enforcement Act (FL-105)

Step 2: File the forms with the Court Clerk

*See Filing Instructions below.

Step 3: Personally service the other spouse

*See Service Instructions below.

Step 4: Complete and file proof of service.

• Proof of Service of Summons (FL-115) for Personal

Service

Respondent

Step 5: Prepare a response to the initial case forms.

Response– Marriage/Domestic Partnership (FL-120)

IF there is a minor child(ren) of the marriage:

• Declaration Under Uniform Child Custody Jurisdiction and Enforcement Act (FL-105)

Step 6: File the forms with the Court Clerk

*See Filing Instructions below.

Step 7: Mail serve the other spouse

*See Service Instructions below

Step 8: Complete and file proof of service.

• Proof of Service by Mail (FL-335).

Stage 2 – Financial Disclosure Forms

Step 9: Each spouse to prepare Financial Disclosures

Declaration of Disclosure (FL-140)

Attach copies of tax returns filed by you for the past two(2) years. (This form *does not* get filed with the Court.)

Schedule of Assets and Debts (FL-142)

Review the form and attach copies of any required deeds, title, statements, etc. (This form *does not* get filed with the Court.)

Income and Expense Declaration (FL-150)

Attach copies of the last two((2) months pay stubs, or if self-employed, Schedule C, from your most recent tax return.

(**IF** there are issues of child support and/or spousal or partner support, then this form **DOES** get filed with the Court.)

Declaration Regarding Service of Declaration of Disclosure (FL-141)

(This form **DOES** get filed with the Court **after** the above forms have been served on the other party.)

Be sure to black out social security numbers on any of the above documents.

Step 10: Serve Financial Disclosures on the other spouse.

Option 1 – Personal Service: Serve the *Financial Disclosure* Forms with

Initial Divorce

Option 2 - Service by Mail: Serve the *Financial Disclosure Forms* by mail

AFTER, *Initial Divorce* forms have been served

*See Service Instructions below

Step 11: Complete and file proof of service.

• Proof of Service by Mail (FL-335).

Step 12: Complete and file Declaration Regarding Service of Declaration of Disclosure.

Declaration Regarding Service of Declaration of Disclosure (FL-141)

Stage 3 – Final Judgment/Trial or Settlement Agreement

Step 13: Negotiate a final settlement

Step 14: Enter a Marital Settlement Agreement or move toward trial. Step 14: Prepare and sign appropriate Judgment forms.

Include if Default-No Response Filed

- Request to Enter Default (FL-165)
- Declaration for Default or Uncontested Dissolution or Legal Separation (FL-170)
- Notice of Entry of Judgement (FL-190)
- *Judgment (FL-180)

Include if Uncontested Default – Response Filed

- Appearance, Stipulation, and Waivers (FL-130)
- Stipulation and Waiver of Final Declaration of Disclosure (FL-144)
- Declaration for Default or Uncontested Dissolution or Legal Separation (FL-170)
- Notice of Entry of Judgement (FL-190)
- *Judgment (FL-180)

Attachments as applicable

- Child Custody and Visitation Order Attachment (FL-341)
- Children's Holiday Schedule Attachment (FL-341(C))
- Joint Legal Custody Attachment (FL-341(E))
- Child Support Information and Order Attachment (FL-342)
- Notice of Rights and Responsibilities (FL-192)
- Spousal Support Attachment (FL-157)
- Property Declarations (FL-160)

Attachments as applicable

*Attach the signed Marital Settlement Agreement to the *Judgment (FL-180)*

Step 15: Submit the Judgment packet to Court for Judge's signature and entry by the Court.

Step 16: CELEBRATE!!

Request for Order

Step 1: Prepare Requests for Order and supporting Declaration.

1. Request for Order (FL-300)

2. Attach Supporting Declaration with detailed statements of requested orders.

Possible Attachments:

1. Child custody or visitation (parenting time)

2. Child Custody and Visitation (Parenting Time) Application Attachment (FL- 311)

3. Children's Holiday Schedule Attachment (FL-341(C))

4. Additional Provisions – Physical Custody Attachment (FL-341(D))

5. Joint Legal Custody Attachment (FL-341(E))

Spousal Support

Spousal or Partner Support Declaration Attachment (FL-157)

Step 2: File the forms with the Court Clerk.

*See Filing Instructions below.

Step 3: Serve the other spouse.

SERVICE OPTIONS:

Option 1 (Personal Service): Personal Service (16 court days before the hearing).

Personal Proof of Service (FL-330)

Option 2 (Service by Mail): Service by Mail (must be mailed 16 court days + 5 calendar days before the hearing):

Proof of Service by Mail (FL-335)

*See Service Instructions below.

Step 4: Complete and file proof of service.

*See Filing Instructions below.

Filing Instructions

1. Take your **Original** Forms, and the **two(2) copies** you made to the court clerk's office at the Courthouse indicated on the top of your paperwork.

2. The court clerk will file, stamp your forms, keep the original, and return the two(2) sets of copies to you (this is known as a "conformed copy").

3. One(1) copy is for your records, and two(1) copy is to serve on the other party

4. The Court will require a filing fee be paid at the time of filing.

5. Fee waivers are granted to certain individuals that qualify under the law.

6. You may go to www.courtifo.ca.gov/forms, select the "fee waiver" option, and complete forms FW-001 and FW-003

Service Instructions

DO NOT SERVE YOUR OWN PAPERS!

Someone 18 years of age or older and not a party to your case must serve forms on the other party then complete the appropriate Proof of Service form to be filed with the Court.

1. Proof of Service of Summons (FL-115)

2. Proof of Service by Mail (FL-335)

3. Personal Proof of Service (FL-330)

4. Declaration Regarding Service of Declaration of Disclosure (FL-141)

5. Have the server complete, sign, and date the appropriate Proof form for filing with the Court.

6. Make one(1) copy of the **completed** appropriate Proof form.

7. Take the original and the copy of the appropriate Proof form to the courthouse and file it with the clerk of the court.

8. The clerk will return a conformed copy to you for your records.

TIPS & TOOLS

"My mission in life is not merely to survive, but to thrive; and to do so with some passion, some compassion, some humor, and some style." -- **Maya Angelou**

- REMOVE EMOTIONS FROM THE LEGAL PROCEEDINGS
- DON'T OVER THINK
- DON'T LISTEN TO ADVICE FROM WELL MEANING FRIENDS AND FAMILY
- DON'T EXPECT MIRACLES
- DON'T EXPECT YOUR SPOUSE TO CHANGE
- HAVE REALISTIC EXPECTATIONS
- ALWAYS TAKE THE HIGH ROAD
- HIDE YOUR BUTTONS
- KEEP A POSITIVE OUTLOOK
- TAKE CARE OF YOURSELF

Imagine yourself armored in a Teflon suit.

~ remember, nothing sticks to Teflon ~ it slides ride off.

You will wear your own version of the Teflon suit throughout the process and cover up all those buttons! Now all the bulls**t they spew at you, just slides right off. Just like, "Wonder Women", she deflected evil powers with the use of her bracelet's. You can get as creative, use your imagination, I mean, it doesn't have to be an ugly Teflon suit, it can be a sexy outfit like Wonder Women and your bling deflects the bulls**t, just sayin'!

Wear a Rubber Band on Your Wrist.

For some time, during the first Stages of my divorce, I wore a rubber band around my wrist, and whenever I felt myself using "Stinkin' Thinkin'" or getting a case of the "Galloping What If's…". I would snap that rubber band on my wrist as a reminder to myself to immediately change my thought process before it starts going down unnecessary rabbit holes. Let me tell you, those mail rubber bands hurt! It won't take long to retrain that "Stinkin' Thinkin'."

~ The type of rubber band used for mail, not your hair. ~

This is a great reminder to stop repeating the same behavior or response.

The definition of the word insanity is to do the same thing repeatedly yet expect a different result. I think it's fairly safe to say; we have all been guilty of this at some point or another.

Hide Your Buttons.

Your spouse knows just how to upset you; so don't give them the reaction they are looking for; don't let them bait you into an argument. Let whatever nasty or disparaging comments they spew at you go in one ear and out the other. Maintain your power and control, wait until you are alone then scream and call him all the names you want.

Your Power Card.

~ Laminated index card with the word "POWER" ~

This is your "Power" card, to be used as a reminder to yourself to reclaim your "POWER" over yourself and to never allow someone else to carry that "POWER" of you again.

When you feel that fear creeping in, maybe due to the actions of your spouse, or your runaway thoughts, or when making decisions, this card is the reminder that you alone have the "POWER" over your life.

Child Custody – Don't Reference Timeshare in terms of Percentage.

When you are requesting child custody with the court; avoid referencing timeshare in terms of a percentage. Once the timeshare is determined, the "percentage" is used tp calculate the amount of child support associated with each parents income and timeshare. When a mediator or judge hears the parent reference the timeshare "percent", often times the intent is lost and it becomes assumed that the underlying motivation is money, child support, rather than the best interest of the child.

DO'S & DON'TS

General DON'T dos...	General DO dos... 😊 😊
Don't react when your spouse tries are intentionally trying to get a rise out of you ("Push Your Buttons")	DO keep the safety of yourself and your children (if any) you're first priority.
Don't engage in tit-for-tat	DO listen to your Divorce Support Professional
Don't participate in toxic communication – no contact may be necessary	DO be proactive
Don't get caught up in the "he said/she said" blame games	DO educate yourself on the process
Don't expect the process to suddenly change your spouse	DO be the best advocate you can be for yourselves

Don't engage in angry texting	DO keep a positive outlook
Don't have a light switch thinking, "Well them I'm just screwed," when something in the divorce process may not seem to go your way.	DO have realistic expectations
Don't take a negative approach to the process of divorce	DO pay attention to your instincts
Don't expect an attorney to have a magic wand and make miracles happen	DO believe in yourself
General DON'T dos...	**General DO dos...** 😊 😊
Don't self-blame	DO be willing to step outside your comfort zone
Don't negotiate against yourself	DO take the high road
Don't make decisions based on of fear	DO keep a sense of humor about things
Don't be an Ostrich with your head in the sand	DO keep the safety of yourself and your children (if any) your first priority.
Don't Underestimate your strength and courage	DO listen to your Divorce Support Professional
Believing and an attorney can magically get you what you want	DO be proactive
Don't have unrealistic expectations	DO educate yourself on the process
Don't have expectations based on what your friends and/or family may have told you.	DO be the best advocate you can be for yourselves
General DON'T dos...	**General DO dos...** 😊 😊
Don't expect your spouse to change	DO have realistic expectations
Don't spend time trying to get a high-conflict spouse to "understand" their bad behavior	DO pay attention to your instincts
Don't "What if..." every possibility	DO believe in yourself
Don't overthink	

LEGAL TERMS & ACRONYMS

"Never let them see you sweat" **– Mary Kennedy**

Term or Acronym	Definition
ATRO'S	Automatic Temporary Restraining Orders on the back of the Summons
BIFURCATION	To separate into two (2) parts – terminate the marriage; then deal with the remaining issues.
CONTESTED	Response no Agreement goes to Trial
CONFORMED COPY	The court returned the file-stamped copy with the date of filing stamped on it.
CCRC	Child Custody Recommending Counseling
DEFAULT	Means No Response Filed
DISCOVERY	The legal process for exchanging information between the parties about witnesses and evidence
DISSOLUTION	Divorce
DVRO	Domestic Violence Restraining Order

EX PARTE	Emergency Hearing
FORM ROGS	Form Interrogatories (An instrument used in the Discovery process.)
I&E	Income and Expense Declaration
ISSUE (CONTEXT)	Children
ISSUE (CONTEXT)	Problem at hand
JURISDICTION	The official power to make legal decisions and judgments.

JOINT CUSTODY	Custody shared by divorced parents.
JURISDICTION	Power of the court to make orders and have them enforced.
LDA	Legal Document Assistant
LEGAL CUSTODY	Gives the parent decision-making rights about raising the minor child(ren) and key aspects involving education, health, safety, and welfare.
MSA	Marital Settlement Agreement
ORDINARY EXPENSES	Costs and expenses for necessities such as food, clothing, and shelter.
OST	Order Shortening Time
PERCENTAGES	Custodial timeshare for each parent; used to calculate child support figures.
PARALEGAL	Works under the direction of an attorney
PARTY	A person involved in a lawsuit.

PERSONAL SERVICE	Hand-Delivery by someone over the age of 18 not a party to this action.
PETITIONER	The first party to file and initial the divorce proceedings Always Petitioner

PAYEE	a person to whom a debt is owed.
PAYOR	a person who owes a debt.
PDD, PDOD's Financials, Disclosures	Preliminary Disclosure Documents
PENDENTE LITE	Latin for "during the litigation."
PERSONAL PROPERTY	All property that is not real estate.
PETITION	The title was given to the first document filed in pursuit of a divorce.
PHYSICAL CUSTODY	The parent with whom the child resides. Depending upon arrangements, it may be joint or sole custody.
PLEADING	A formal written application to the the court which requests action by the court.
POST JUDGMENT LITIGATION	Motion-based litigation that follows a final judgment by a court.
POSTNUPTIAL	A written contract between husband and wife states all of their present and future rights given their impending divorce.
PRO PER OR PROPRIA PERSONA	TO REPRESENT YOURSELF
PROCESS SERVER	A professional people finder that serves legal documents.

PUBLIC RECORDS	Records and information in any form in the public domain and open to inspection.
PURPOSE OF AN APPRAISAL	It states the scope of an appraisal assignment, i.e., to estimate a defined value of any real property interest or to conduct an evaluation study about real property decisions.
QUASH	Cancel or limit the scope of a procedure, such as discovery.
QUALIFIED DOMESTIC RELAT-IONS ORDER (QDRO)	A court order stating that a portion of one spouse's pension be awarded to the

another spouse as part of the equitable distribution of the marital assets. |
REAL PROPERTY	All interests, benefits, and rights are inherent in the ownership of the physical real estate.
RESERVED ISSUES	Issues to be decided at a later time.
RFO	Request for Order
RESPONDENT	The second party to file responding to the divorce proceedings Always Respondent
SAD	Schedule of Assets & Debts
SERVICE	Delivery of a legal document by someone over the age of 18 and not a party involved in the legal case.
SPOUSAL SUPPORT	Support intended to help the ex-spouse become financially self-sufficient.
SANCTIONS	a money award to punish a party for egregiously bad behavior.
SECRETION OF ASSETS	The hiding of assets.

SEPARATE PROPERTY	Property is considered to be owned by one spouse before marriage, which in most states is not up for a divorce.
SEPARATION	When spouses no longer live together as a married couple
SET ASIDE	To cancel, annul, or revoke a prior judgment of a court.

SUBPOENA	A document that is delivered to a person who is not directly involved in the action filed but is in need for testimony.
SUBPOENA DUCES TECUM	A court order to produce documents as part of discovery; subpoena duces tecum means "bring with you."
SUBPOENA AD TESTIFICAN-DUM	A court order requiring a person to testify at a trial or give testimony at a deposition.
SUBSTITUTION OF AN ATTORNEY	A special pleading by which a court confirms a party's change in or out of legal representation.
SUMMONS	A written notification to the defendant or respondent that an action has been filed against him or her.
TEMPORARY CUSTODY	A spouse's right to have parenting time with his or her child. It includes extended stays and overnights.
TEMPORARY RESTRAINING ORDER	An order of the court prohibiting a party from acting, for example, threatening, harassing, or physically abusing the other spouse and/or the children; selling personal property; taking money out of accounts; denying the other spouse's motor vehicle.

TEMPORARY SUPPORT	An interlocutory order of support entered before the trial, issued while a case is pending.
TOLLING	An artificial stop in time so that the statute of limitation does not expire and thus prohibits litigation.
TRACING	What do courts do to identify separate and marital property?
TRO	Temporary Restraining Order
UCCJEA	The Uniform Child Custody Jurisdiction and Enforcement Act, a uniform law regarding custody and visitation for parties from different states.
UNCONTESTED	Response filed with an Agreement

UIFSA	The Uniform Interstate Family Support Act, a new uniform law regarding child support and alimony for parties from different states.
UNIFORM PARENTAGE ACT of 2000 (UPA)	Deals with new reproductive technologies and the problems caused by the late discovery of paternity.
WAGE ASSIGNMENT OR WAGE WITHHOLDING	A court order requiring the employer of a noncustodial parent to deduct a specific amount of money for child support from the wages of the noncustodial parent (also known as garnishment).
WAIVER	A written document that relinquishes an individual's rights.

WELFARE	A popular name for Aid to Families with Dependent Children (AFDC) and Temporary Assistance for Needy Families (TANF).
WITH PREJUDICE	Something decided, ordered, adjudged, without the opportunity to refile.
WITHOUT PREJUDICE	Something decided, ordered, adjudged, but settled in a way the parties may refile.
WITNESS	A person knows facts or other information about a specific situation.

RESOURCES

"When we deny our stories, They define us. When we own our stories, we get to write the ending." – **Brené Brown**

Co-Parenting Apps

Talking Parents: Talkingparents.org

Our Family Wizard: Ourfamilywizard.com

Coaching Support

Laila Aitken Ali – The Split Coach
@laila_thesplitcoach

Heather Steer – CDFA
https://divorcetransitionmentors.com/

Maddie Mackey – Rise Above Yoga
Trauma Recovery
Riseaboveyoga.com

Help Hotlines

National Suicide Prevention Lifeline: 1-800-273-TALK (8255)

National Domestic Violence Hotline: 1-800-799-SAFE (7233)

Family Violence Prevention Center: 1-800-313-1310

Battered Women and their Children: 1-800-603-HELP

Safe Alternatives for Everyone (SAFE)
Safefamiliesca.org

Podcasts

Split.fyi Coffee Talk

Support Groups

Splity.fyi @splitfyi
Alcoholics Anonymous: aa.org Narcotics
Anonymous: na.org

Self-Care Suggestions

Helpful Books

Journal

Schedule a daily walk Headspace.com

Les Brown on You Tube Motivational Speeches on You Tube TED Talks on You Tube

COMPLETING, FILING & SERVING FORMS

"I have not ceased being fearful, but I have ceased to let fear control me."

—Erica Jong

PETITIONER CHECKLIST and INSTRUCTIONS

DIVORCE FORMS CHECKLIST	
Initial Filing forms	Financial Disclosure forms
Summons (FL-110)	Income and Expense Declaration (FL-150)
Petition (FL-100)	Schedule of Assets and Debts (FL-142)
Declaration of Residence (RI-FL-036)	Declaration of Disclosure (FL-140)

Declaration Under Uniform Child Custody Jurisdiction and Enforcement Act (FL-105) (*if the minor child(ren)*)	Declaration Regarding Service of Declaration of Disclosure (FL-141)

*Blank Forms to Be Served on Other Party (see Service Instructions).

PROOF(s) OF SERVICE	PROOF(s) OF SERVICE
Personal Proof of Service (FL-115)	Proof of Service by Mail (FL-335)
*See filing instructions for Proof(s) of Service.	

Instructions

REVIEW	SIGN and DATE
After you have completed your forms, be sure To **REVIEW EACH FORM FOR ACCURACY.**	Be sure to sign and date each form where indicated.

COPY FORMS	FILING YOUR PAPERS with the COURT
Make two (2) copies of each form. One (1) copy will be for your records One (1) copy will be served on the other party.	Take the **ORIGINAL and TWO (2) COPIES** to the court clerk's office in the County of your filing. The court clerk will file, stamp the forms, keep the original and return the two (2) sets of copies to you.

COURT FEES

The Court will require a filing fee be paid at the time of filing	Fee waivers are granted to certain individuals that qualify under the law. You may go to www.courtinfo.ca.gov/forms, select the "fee waiver" option, and complete forms FW-001 and FW-003.
PERSONAL SERVICE on OTHER PARTY	SERVICE BY MAIL on OTHER PARTY
One (1) set of copies **AND** the **BLANK FORMS** *must* be PERSONALLY served to the opposing party. Service can be done by a Process Server or by someone over the age of 18 years of age and not a party to this case. **DO NOT SERVE OUR OWN PAPERS**	One (1) set of copies **AND** the **BLANK FORMS** *must* be PERSONALLY served to the opposing party. Service can be done by a Process Server or by someone over the age of 18 years of age and not a party to this case. **DO NOT SERVE OUR PAPERS.**

RESPONDENT CHECKLIST and INSTRUCTIONS

DIVORCE FORMS CHECKLIST	
Initial Filing forms	**Financial Disclosure forms**
Response (FL-120)	Income and Expense Declaration (FL-150)
Declaration Under Uniform Child Custody Jurisdiction and Enforcement Act (FL-105) (*if the minor child(ren)*)	Schedule of Assets and Debts (FL-142)
	Declaration of Disclosure (FL-140)
	Declaration Regarding Service of Declaration of Disclosure (FL-141)
The Response may be served by U.S. Mail.	
PROOF(s) OF SERVICE	**PROOF(s) OF SERVICE**
Proof of Service by Mail (FL-335)	Proof of Service by Mail (FL-335)
*See filing instructions for Proof(s) of Service.	
Instructions	
REVIEW	SIGN and DATE
After you have completed your forms, be sure To **REVIEW EACH FORM FOR ACCURACY.**	Be sure to sign and date each form where indicated.

COPY FORMS	FILING YOUR PAPERS with the COURT
Make two (2) copies of each form. One (1) copy will be for your records One (1) copy will be served on the other party.	Take the **ORIGINAL and TWO (2) COPIES** to the court clerk's office in the County of your filing. The court clerk will file, stamp the forms, keep the original and return the two (2) sets of copies to you.
COURT FEES	
The Court will require a filing fee be paid at the time of filing	Fee waivers are granted to certain individuals that qualify under the law. You may go to www.courtinfo.ca.gov/forms, select the "fee waiver" option, and complete forms FW-001 and FW-003.
PERSONAL SERVICE on OTHER PARTY	SERVICE BY MAIL on OTHER PARTY
One (1) set of copies **AND** the **BLANK FORMS** *must* be PERSONALLY served on the opposing party. Service can be done by a Process Server or by someone over the age of 18 years of age	One (1) set of copies **AND** the **BLANK FORMS** *must* be PERSONALLY served on the opposing party. Service can be done by a Process Server or by someone over the age of 18 years of age

and not a party to this case. **DO NOT SERVE OUR OWN PAPERS**	and not a party to this case. **DO NOT SERVE OUR PAPERS.**

EXAMPLE DIVORCE FORMS

In Re the Marriage of Barry D. and Ima Dunn Hatchett

"The weak can never forgive. Forgiveness is the attribute of the strong." **– Mahatma Gandhi**

To help understand the flow of the forms and the legal process, you can reference completed form examples using the following hypothetical information over the next few pages.

Case Information:

Parties:	Statistical Facts
Petitioner: Ima Dunn Hatchet Address: 234 Rocky Road Splitsville, CA 95785 Respondent: Barry D. Hatchet Address: 789 Memory Lane Sunny, CA 95785	Date of Marriage: October 10, 2000 Date of Separation: January 22, 2021 Length of Marriage: 20 years, 2 months
Minor Children:	**Issues of Contention**
Kay Oss Hatchet, date of birth, 03/21/2017, age 3, daughter Upton O'Good Hatchet, date of birth 03/02/2014, age 6, son	Child Custody Child Support Spousal Support Sale of Marital Residence

SUPERIOR COURT OF CALIFORNIA, COUNTY OF RIVERSIDE

☐ **BLYTHE** 265 N. Broadway, Blythe, CA 92225
☐ **HEMET** 880 N. State St., Hemet, CA 92543

☐ **INDIO** 46-200 Oasis St., Indio, CA 92201
☑ **RIVERSIDE** 4175 Main St., Riverside, CA 92501

RI-FL036

ATTORNEY OR PARTY WITHOUT ATTORNEY (Name, State Bar number and Address) Ima Dunn Hatchet In Pro Per 1234 Rocky Road Splitsville CA 92395 TELEPHONE NO. 951-555-1212 FAX NO. (Optional): E-MAIL ADDRESS (Optional): SamPull@gmail.com ATTORNEY FOR (Name): Ima Dunn Hatchet	FOR COURT USE ONLY
PETITIONER: Ima Dunn Hatchet	
RESPONDENT: Barry D. Hatchet	
	CASE NUMBER:

DECLARATION OF RESIDENCE

The undersigned certifies that this case should be tried or heard in the:

☐ Blythe Court   ☐ Hemet Court   ☐ Indio Court   ☑ Riverside Court

for the following reasons:

☐ The party's primary residence is located within the geographical area. The city and zip code is:

City Splitsville   Zip Code   92395

☐ Other:

I declare under penalty of perjury under the laws of the State of California that the information above is true and correct.

Date: 03/20/2021

Ima Dunn Hatchet

Ima Dunn Hatchet
(TYPE OR PRINT NAME OF   ☐ ATTORNEY   ☐ PARTY MAKING DECLARATION)   (SIGNATURE)

Page 1 of 1

Adopted for Mandatory Use
Riverside Superior Court
RI-FL036 [Rev. 01/01/13]

DECLARATION OF RESIDENCE

www.courts.ca.gov/forms www.courtinfo.ca.gov

FL-110

SUMMONS (Family Law)

CITACIÓN (Derecho familiar)

NOTICE TO RESPONDENT *(Name):* Barry D. Hatchet
AVISO AL DEMANDADO (Nombre):

You have been sued. Read the information below and on the next page.
Lo han demandado. Lea la información a continuación y en la página siguiente.

Petitioner's name ia: Ima Dunn Hatchet
Nombre del demandante:

CASE NUMBER *(NÚMERO DE CASO):*

You have 30 calendar days after this *Summons* and *Petition* are served on you to file a *Response* (form FL-120) at the court and have a copy served on the petitioner. A letter, phone call, or court appearance will not protect you.	*Tiene 30 días de calendario después de haber recibido la entrega legal de esta Citación y Petición para presentar una Respuesta (formulario FL-120) ante la corte y efectuar la entrega legal de una copia al demandante. Una carta o una llamada telefónica o una audiencia de la corte no basta para protegerlo.*
If you do not file your *Response* on time, the court may make orders affecting your marriage or domestic partnership, your property, and custody of your children. You may be ordered to pay support and attorney fees and costs.	*Si no presenta su Respuesta a tiempo, la corte puede dar órdenes que afecten su matrimonio o pareja de hecho, sus bienes y la custodia de sus hijos. La corte también le puede ordenar que pague manutención, y honorarios y costos legales.*
For legal advice, contact a lawyer immediately. Get help finding a lawyer at the California Courts Online Self-Help Center (www.courts.ca.gov/selfhelp), at the California Legal Services website (www.lawhelpca.org), or by contacting your local county bar association.	*Para asesoramiento legal, póngase en contacto de inmediato con un abogado. Puede obtener información para encontrar un abogado en el Centro de Ayuda de las Cortes de California (www.sucorte.ca.gov), en el sitio web de los Servicios Legales de California (www.lawhelpca.org) o poniéndose en contacto con el colegio de abogados de su condado.*
NOTICE—RESTRAINING ORDERS ARE ON PAGE 2: These restraining orders are effective against both spouses or domestic partners until the petition is dismissed, a judgment is entered, or the court makes further orders. They are enforceable anywhere in California by any law enforcement officer who has received or seen a copy of them.	*AVISO—LAS ÓRDENES DE RESTRICCIÓN SE ENCUENTRAN EN LA PÁGINA 2: Las órdenes de restricción están en vigencia en cuanto a ambos cónyuges o miembros de la pareja de hecho hasta que se despida la petición, se emita un fallo o la corte dé otras órdenes. Cualquier agencia del orden público que haya recibido o visto una copia de estas órdenes puede hacerlas acatar en cualquier lugar de California.*
FEE WAIVER: If you cannot pay the filing fee, ask the clerk for a fee waiver form. The court may order you to pay back all or part of the fees and costs that the court waived for you or the other party.	*EXENCIÓN DE CUOTAS: Si no puede pagar la cuota de presentación, pida al secretario un formulario de exención de cuotas. La corte puede ordenar que usted pague, ya sea en parte o por completo, las cuotas y costos de la corte previamente exentos a petición de usted o de la otra parte.*

[SEAL]

1. The name and address of the court are *(El nombre y dirección de la corte son):*
   Hemet Courthouse
   880 N. State Street
   Hemet CA 92543

2. The name, address, and telephone number of the petitioner's attorney, or the petitioner without an attorney, are: *(El nombre, dirección y número de teléfono del abogado del demandante, o del demandante si no tiene abogado, son):*
   Ima Dunn Hatchet
   In Pro Per
   1234 Rocky Road Splitsville CA 92395
   951-555-1212

Date *(Fecha):* _____ Clerk , by *(Secretario, por)* _____ , Deputy *(Asistente)* _____

Page 1 of 2

Form Adopted for Mandatory Use
Judicial Council of California
FL-110 [Rev. January 1, 2018]

SUMMONS
(Family Law)

Family Code, §§ 232, 233, 2024.7, 2040, 7700;
Code of Civ. Procedure, §§ 412.20, 416.60–416.90
www.courts.ca.gov

STANDARD FAMILY LAW RESTRAINING ORDERS

Starting immediately, you and your spouse or domestic partner are restrained from:

1. removing the minor children of the parties from the state or applying for a new or replacement passport for those minor children without the prior written consent of the other party or an order of the court;

2. cashing, borrowing against, canceling, transferring, disposing of, or changing the beneficiaries of any insurance or other coverage, including life, health, automobile, and disability, held for the benefit of the parties and their minor children;

3. transferring, encumbering, hypothecating, concealing, or in any way disposing of any property, real or personal, whether community, quasi-community, or separate, without the written consent of the other party or an order of the court, except in the usual course of business or for the necessities of life; and

4. creating a nonprobate transfer or modifying a nonprobate transfer in a manner that affects the disposition of property subject to the transfer, without the written consent of the other party or an order of the court. Before revocation of a nonprobate transfer can take effect or a right of survivorship to property can be eliminated, notice of the change must be filed and served on the other party.

You must notify each other of any proposed extraordinary expenditures at least five business days prior to incurring these extraordinary expenditures and account to the court for all extraordinary expenditures made after these restraining orders are effective. However, you may use community property, quasi-community property, or your own separate property to pay an attorney to help you or to pay court costs.

NOTICE—ACCESS TO AFFORDABLE HEALTH INSURANCE:
Do you or someone in your household need affordable health insurance? If so, you should apply for Covered California. Covered California can help reduce the cost you pay towards high quality affordable health care. For more information, visit www.coveredca.com. Or call Covered California at 1-800-300-1506.

WARNING—IMPORTANT INFORMATION

California law provides that, for purposes of division of property upon dissolution of a marriage or domestic partnership or upon legal separation, property acquired by the parties during marriage or domestic partnership in joint form is presumed to be community property. If either party to this action should die before the jointly held community property is divided, the language in the deed that characterizes how title is held (i.e., joint tenancy, tenants in common, or community property) will be controlling, and not the community property presumption. You should consult your attorney if you want the community property presumption to be written into the recorded title to the property.

ÓRDENES DE RESTRICCIÓN ESTÁNDAR DE DERECHO FAMILIAR

En forma inmediata, usted y su cónyuge o pareja de hecho tienen prohibido:

1. llevarse del estado de California a los hijos menores de las partes, o solicitar un pasaporte nuevo o de repuesto para los hijos menores, sin el consentimiento previo por escrito de la otra parte o sin una orden de la corte;

2. cobrar, pedir prestado, cancelar, transferir, deshacerse o cambiar el nombre de los beneficiarios de cualquier seguro u otro tipo de cobertura, como de vida, salud, vehículo y discapacidad, que tenga como beneficiario(s) a las partes y su(s) hijo(s) menor(es);

3. transferir, gravar, hipotecar, ocultar o deshacerse de cualquier manera de cualquier propiedad, inmueble o personal, ya sea comunitaria, cuasicomunitaria o separada, sin el consentimiento escrito de la otra parte o una orden de la corte, excepto en el curso habitual de actividades personales y comerciales o para satisfacer las necesidades de la vida; y

4. crear o modificar una transferencia no testamentaria de manera que afecte la asignación de una propiedad sujeta a transferencia, sin el consentimiento por escrito de la otra parte o una orden de la corte. Antes de que se pueda eliminar la revocación de una transferencia no testamentaria, se debe presentar ante la corte un aviso del cambio y hacer una entrega legal de dicho aviso a la otra parte.

Cada parte tiene que notificar a la otra sobre cualquier gasto extraordinario propuesto por lo menos cinco días hábiles antes de realizarlo, y rendir cuenta a la corte de todos los gastos extraordinarios realizados después de que estas órdenes de restricción hayan entrado en vigencia. No obstante, puede usar propiedad comunitaria, cuasicomunitaria o suya separada para pagar a un abogado que lo ayude o para pagar los costos de la corte.

AVISO—ACCESO A SEGURO DE SALUD MÁS ECONÓMICO:
¿Necesita seguro de salud a un costo asequible, ya sea para usted o alguien en su hogar? Si es así, puede presentar una solicitud con Covered California. Covered California lo puede ayudar a reducir el costo que paga por seguro de salud asequible y de alta calidad. Para obtener más información, visite www.coveredca.com. O llame a Covered California al 1-800-300-0213.

ADVERTENCIA—IMFORMACIÓN IMPORTANTE

De acuerdo a la ley de California, las propiedades adquiridas por las partes durante su matrimonio o pareja de hecho en forma conjunta se consideran propiedad comunitaria para fines de la división de bienes que ocurre cuando se produce una disolución o separación legal del matrimonio o pareja de hecho. Si cualquiera de las partes de este caso llega a fallecer antes de que se divida la propiedad comunitaria de tenencia conjunta, el destino de la misma quedará determinado por las cláusulas de la escritura correspondiente que describen su tenencia (por ej., tenencia conjunta, tenencia en común o propiedad comunitaria) y no por la presunción de propiedad comunitaria. Si quiere que la presunción comunitaria quede registrada en la escritura de la propiedad, debería consultar con un abogado.

SUMMONS
(Family Law)

FL-100

PARTY WITHOUT ATTORNEY OR ATTORNEY	STATE BAR NUMBER:	FOR COURT USE ONLY
NAME: Ima Dunn Hatchet		
FIRM NAME: In Pro Per		
STREET ADDRESS: 1234 Rocky Road		
CITY: Splitsville STATE: CA ZIP CODE: 92395		
TELEPHONE NO.: 951-555-1212 FAX NO.:		
E-MAIL ADDRESS: SamPull@gmail.com		
ATTORNEY FOR (name): Ima Dunn Hatchet		

SUPERIOR COURT OF CALIFORNIA, COUNTY OF Riverside
STREET ADDRESS:880 N. State Street
MAILING ADDRESS:880 N. State Street
CITY AND ZIP CODE: Hemet 92543
BRANCH NAME: Hemet Courthouse

PETITIONER: Ima Dunn Hatchet
RESPONDENT: Barry D. Hatchet

PETITION FOR		☐ AMENDED	CASE NUMBER:
✔ **Dissolution (Divorce)** of:	✔ Marriage	☐ Domestic Partnership	
☐ **Legal Separation** of:	☐ Marriage	☐ Domestic Partnership	
☐ **Nullity** of:	☐ Marriage	☐ Domestic Partnership	

1. **LEGAL RELATIONSHIP** (check all that apply):
   a. ✔ We are married.
   b. ☐ We are domestic partners and our domestic partnership was established in California.
   c. ☐ We are domestic partners and our domestic partnership was NOT established in California.

2. **RESIDENCE REQUIREMENTS** (check all that apply):
   a. ✔ Petitioner ✔ Respondent has been a resident of this state for at least six months and of this county for at least three months immediately preceding the filing of this Petition. (For a divorce, unless you are in the legal relationship described in 1b., at least one of you must comply with this requirement.)
   b. ☐ Our domestic partnership was established in California. Neither of us has to be a resident or have a domicile in California to dissolve our partnership here.
   c. ☐ We are the same sex, were married in California, but currently live in a jurisdiction that does not recognize, and will not dissolve, our marriage. This Petition is filed in the county where we married.
   Petitioner lives in (specify):   Respondent lives in (specify):

3. **STATISTICAL FACTS**
   a. ✔ (1) Date of marriage (specify): 10/10/2000   (2) Date of separation (specify): 01/22/2021
      (3) Time from date of marriage to date of separation (specify): 20   Years 2   Months
   b. ☐ (1) Registration date of domestic partnership with the California Secretary of State or other state equivalent (specify below):
      (2) Date of separation (specify):
      (3) Time from date of registration of domestic partnership to date of separation (specify):   Years   Months

4. **MINOR CHILDREN**
   a. ☐ There are no minor children.
   b. ✔ The minor children are:

Child's name	Birthdate	Age
Kay Oss Hatchet	03/21/2017	3 yrs
Upton O'Goode Hatchet	09/19/2014	6 yrs

   (1) ☐ continued on Attachment 4b.   (2) ☐ a child who is not yet born.
   c. If any children listed above were born before the marriage or domestic partnership, the court has the authority to determine those children to be children of the marriage or domestic partnership.
   d. If there are minor children of Petitioner and Respondent, a completed Declaration Under Uniform Child Custody Jurisdiction and Enforcement Act (UCCJEA) (form FL-105) must be attached.
   e. ☐ Petitioner and Respondent signed a voluntary declaration of parentage or paternity. (Attach a copy if available.)

Page 1 of 3

Form Adopted for Mandatory Use
Judicial Council of California
FL-100 [Rev. January 1, 2020]

PETITION—MARRIAGE/DOMESTIC PARTNERSHIP
(Family Law)

Family Code, §§ 297, 299, 2320, 2330, 3409
www.courts.ca.gov

FL-100

		CASE NUMBER:
PETITIONER:	Ima Dunn Hatchet	
RESPONDENT:	Barry D. Hatchet	

Petitioner requests that the court make the following orders:

5. **LEGAL GROUNDS** (Family Code sections 2200–2210. 2310–2312)
   a. ☑ Divorce or ☐ Legal separation of the marriage or domestic partnership based on *(check one):*
       (1) ☑ irreconcilable differences.   (2) ☐ permanent legal incapacity to make decisions.
   b. ☐ Nullity of void marriage or domestic partnership based on
       (1) ☐ incest.   (2) ☐ bigamy.
   c. ☐ Nullity of voidable marriage or domestic partnership based on
       (1) ☐ petitioner's age at time of registration of domestic   (4) ☐ fraud.
           partnership or marriage.
       (2) ☐ prior existing marriage or domestic partnership.   (5) ☐ force.
       (3) ☐ unsound mind.   (6) ☐ physical incapacity.

6. **CHILD CUSTODY AND VISITATION (PARENTING TIME)**

	Petitioner	Respondent	Joint	Other
a. Legal custody of children to	☐	☐	☑	☐
b. Physical custody of children to	☐	☐	☑	☐
c. Child visitation (parenting time) be granted to	☐	☐		☐

    As requested in   ☐ form FL-311   ☐ form FL-312   ☐ form FL-341(C)
                  ☐ form FL-341(D)   ☐ form FL-341(E)   ☐ Attachment 6c(1)

7. **CHILD SUPPORT**
   a. If there are minor children born to or adopted by Petitioner and Respondent before or during this marriage or domestic partnership, the court will make orders for the support of the children upon request and submission of financial forms by the requesting party.
   b. An earnings assignment may be issued without further notice.
   c. Any party required to pay support must pay interest on overdue amounts at the "legal" rate, which is currently 10 percent.
   d. ☐ Other *(specify):*

8. **SPOUSAL OR DOMESTIC PARTNER SUPPORT**
   a. ☑ Spousal or domestic partner support payable to ☑ Petitioner ☐ Respondent
   b. ☑ Terminate (end) the court's ability to award support to ☐ Petitioner ☑ Respondent
   c. ☐ Reserve for future determination the issue of support payable to ☐ Petitioner ☐ Respondent
   d. ☐ Other *(specify):*

9. **SEPARATE PROPERTY**
   a. ☐ There are no such assets or debts that I know of to be confirmed by the court.
   b. ☑ Confirm as separate property the assets and debts in ☐ *Property Declaration* (form FL-160). ☐ Attachment 9b.
       ☑ the following list.   Item   Confirm to
       All acquisitions before marriage and post-separation and all gifts, and the balance of the
       assets and obligations, separate or otherwise, are unknown to Petitioner who will amend
       these pleadings once ascertained or according to proof at the time of Trial.

PETITION—MARRIAGE/DOMESTIC PARTNERSHIP
(Family Law)

FL-100

PETITIONER:	Ima Dunn Hatchet	CASE NUMBER:
RESPONDENT:	Barry D. Hatchet	

10. COMMUNITY AND QUASI-COMMUNITY PROPERTY

    a. ☐ There are no such assets or debts that I know of to be divided by the court.

    b. ☑ Determine rights to community and quasi-community assets and debts. All such assets and debts are listed

        ☐ in *Property Declaration* (form FL-160)   ☐ in Attachment 10b.

        ☑ as follows *(specify)*:

        Real property; motor vehicles; furniture; furnishings and appliances; debts;

        retirement accounts; financial accounts; and the balance of the assets and obligations, community or

        otherwise, are unknown to Petitioner who will amend these pleadings once ascertained or according to

        proof at time of Trial

11. OTHER REQUESTS

    a. ☑ Attorney's fees and costs payable by   ☐ Petitioner   ☑ Respondent

    b. ☑ Petitioner's former name be restored to *(specify)*: Dunn

    c. ☐ Other *(specify)*:

    ☐ Continued on Attachment 11c.

12. I HAVE READ THE RESTRAINING ORDERS ON THE BACK OF THE SUMMONS, AND I UNDERSTAND THAT THEY APPLY TO ME WHEN THIS PETITION IS FILED.

I declare under penalty of perjury under the laws of the State of California that the foregoing is true and correct.

Date: 03/20/2021

Ima Dunn Hatchet   *Ima Dunn Hatchet*
      (TYPE OR PRINT NAME)   (SIGNATURE OF PETITIONER)

Date:

Ima Dunn Hatchet
      (TYPE OR PRINT NAME)   (SIGNATURE OF ATTORNEY FOR PETITIONER)

FOR MORE INFORMATION: Read *Legal Steps for a Divorce or Legal Separation* (**form FL-107-INFO**) and visit "Families Change" at *www.familieschange.ca.gov* — an online guide for parents and children going through divorce or separation.

NOTICE: You may redact (black out) social security numbers from any written material filed with the court in this case other than a form used to collect child, spousal or partner support.

NOTICE—CANCELLATION OF RIGHTS: Dissolution or legal separation may automatically cancel the rights of a domestic partner or spouse under the other domestic partner's or spouse's will, trust, retirement plan, power of attorney, pay-on-death bank account, survivorship rights to any property owned in joint tenancy, and any other similar thing. It does not automatically cancel the right of a domestic partner or spouse as beneficiary of the other partner's or spouse's life insurance policy. You should review these matters, as well as any credit cards, other credit accounts, insurance polices, retirement plans, and credit reports, to determine whether they should be changed or whether you should take any other actions. Some changes may require the agreement of your partner or spouse or a court order.

FL-105/GC-120

ATTORNEY OR PARTY WITHOUT ATTORNEY *(Name, State Bar number, and address)*	FOR COURT USE ONLY
Ima Dunn Hatchet In Pro Per 1234 Rocky Road Splitsville CA 92395 TELEPHONE NO.: 951-555-1212 FAX NO. *(Optional):* E-MAIL ADDRESS *(Optional):* SamPull@gmail.com ATTORNEY FOR *(Name):* Ima Dunn Hatchet	

SUPERIOR COURT OF CALIFORNIA, COUNTY OF Riverside
STREET ADDRESS: 880 N. State Street
MAILING ADDRESS:
CITY AND ZIP CODE: Hemet 92543
BRANCH NAME: Hemet Courthouse

(This section applies only to family law cases.)
PETITIONER: Ima Dunn Hatchet
RESPONDENT: Barry D. Hatchet
OTHER PARTY:

(This section applies only to guardianship cases.)
GUARDIANSHIP OF *(Name):*   Minor

CASE NUMBER:
XYZ123456

**DECLARATION UNDER UNIFORM CHILD CUSTODY
JURISDICTION AND ENFORCEMENT ACT (UCCJEA)**

1. **I am a party** to this proceeding to determine custody of a child.

2. ☐ My present address and the present address of each child residing with me is confidential under Family Code section 3429 as I have indicated in item 3.

3. There are *(specify number):*   minor children who are subject to this proceeding, as follows:
(Insert the information requested below. The residence information must be given for the last FIVE years.)

a. Child's name	Place of birth	Date of birth	Sex
Kay Oss Hatchet	Sunny, CA	03/21/2017	Female

Period of residence	Address 1234 Rocky Road Splittsville, CA Califc 95786 ☐ Confidential	Person child lived with *(name and complete current address)* Ima Dunn ☐ Confidential	Relationship Mother
03/08/2020 to present	Child's residence *(City, State)* 789 Memory Lane, Sunny, CA 98765	Person child lived with *(name and complete current address)* Ima Dunn and Barry D. Hatchet	Mother & Father
12/23/20 to 03/08/202(	Child's residence *(City, State)*	Person child lived with *(name and complete current address)*	
to	Child's residence *(City, State)*	Person child lived with *(name and complete current address)*	

b. Child's name	Place of birth	Date of birth	Sex
Upton O'Good Hatchet ☑ Residence information is the same as given above for child a. *(If NOT the same, provide the information below.)*	Sunny, CA	09/19/2014	Male

Period of residence	Address ☐ Confidential	Person child lived with *(name and complete current address)* ☐ Confidential	Relationship
to present	Child's residence *(City, State)*	Person child lived with *(name and complete current address)*	
to	Child's residence *(City, State)*	Person child lived with *(name and complete current address)*	
to	Child's residence *(City, State)*	Person child lived with *(name and complete current address)*	

c. ☐ Additional residence information for a child listed in item a or b is continued on attachment 3c.

d. ☐ Additional children are listed on form FL-105(A)/GC-120(A). *(Provide all requested information for additional children.)*

Page 1 of 2

Form Adopted for Mandatory Use
Judicial Council of California
FL-105/GC-120 [Rev. January 1, 2009]

**DECLARATION UNDER UNIFORM CHILD CUSTODY
JURISDICTION AND ENFORCEMENT ACT (UCCJEA)**

Family Code, § 3400 et seq.
Probate Code, §§ 1510(f), 1512
www.courtinfo.ca.gov

FL-105/GC-120

SHORT TITLE:	CASE NUMBER:
In Re Marriage of Hatchet; Ima Dunn & Barry D.	XYZ123456

4. Do you have information about, or have you participated as a party or as a witness or in some other capacity in, another court case or custody or visitation proceeding, in California or elsewhere, concerning a child subject to this proceeding?
   ☐ Yes ☑ No *(If yes, attach a copy of the orders (if you have one) and provide the following information):*

Proceeding	Case number	Court *(name, state, location)*	Court order or judgment *(date)*	Name of each child	Your connection to the case	Case status
a. ☐ Family						
b. ☐ Guardianship						
c. ☐ Other						

Proceeding	Case Number	Court *(name, state, location)*
d. ☐ Juvenile Delinquency/ Juvenile Dependency		
e. ☐ Adoption		

5. ☐ One or more domestic violence restraining/protective orders are now in effect. *(Attach a copy of the orders if you have one and provide the following information):*

Court	County	State	Case number *(if known)*	Orders expire *(date)*
a. ☐ Criminal				
b. ☐ Family				
c. ☐ Juvenile Delinquency/ Juvenile Dependency				
d. ☐ Other				

6. Do you know of any person who is not a party to this proceeding who has physical custody or claims to have custody of or visitation rights with any child in this case? ☐ Yes ☑ No *(If yes, provide the following information):*

a. Name and address of person	b. Name and address of person	c. Name and address of person
☐ Has physical custody ☐ Claims custody rights ☐ Claims visitation rights	☐ Has physical custody ☐ Claims custody rights ☐ Claims visitation rights	☐ Has physical custody ☐ Claims custody rights ☐ Claims visitation rights
Name of each child	Name of each child	Name of each child

I declare under penalty of perjury under the laws of the State of California that the foregoing is true and correct.
Date: 03/20/2021

Ima Dunn Hatchet

Ima Dunn Hatchet
_____
(TYPE OR PRINT NAME)

► _____
(SIGNATURE OF DECLARANT)

7. ☑ Number of pages attached: 0

NOTICE TO DECLARANT: You have a continuing duty to inform this court if you obtain any information about a custody proceeding in a California court or any other court concerning a child subject to this proceeding.

FL-105/GC-120 [Rev. January 1, 2009]

**DECLARATION UNDER UNIFORM CHILD CUSTODY
JURISDICTION AND ENFORCEMENT ACT (UCCJEA)**

Page 2 of 2

FL-115

PARTY WITHOUT ATTORNEY or ATTORNEY STATE BAR NO.: NAME: **Ima Dunn Hatchet** FIRM NAME: **In Pro Per** STREET ADDRESS: **1234 Rocky Road** CITY: **Splitsville** STATE: **CA** ZIP CODE: **92395** TELEPHONE NO.: **951-555-1212** FAX NO.: E-MAIL ADDRESS: **SamPull@gmail.com** ATTORNEY FOR (name): **Ima Dunn Hatchet**	FOR COURT USE ONLY
SUPERIOR COURT OF CALIFORNIA, COUNTY OF **Riverside** STREET ADDRESS: **880 N. State Street** MAILING ADDRESS: CITY AND ZIP CODE: **Hemet 92543** BRANCH NAME: **Hemet Courthouse**	

PETITIONER: Ima Dunn Hatchet

RESPONDENT: Barry D. Hatchet

PROOF OF SERVICE OF SUMMONS	CASE NUMBER: **XYZ123456**

1. At the time of service I was at least 18 years of age and not a party to this action. **I served the respondent with copies of:**
   a. ☑ Family Law: *Petition—Marriage/Domestic Partnership* (form FL-100), *Summons* (form FL-110), and blank *Response—Marriage/Domestic Partnership* (form FL-120)
   —or—
   b. ☐ Uniform Parentage: *Petition to Determine Parental Relationship* (form FL-200), *Summons* (form FL-210), and blank *Response to Petition to Determine Parental Relationship* (form FL-220)
   —or—
   c. ☐ Custody and Support: *Petition for Custody and Support of Minor Children* (form FL-260), *Summons* (form FL-210), and blank *Response to Petition for Custody and Support of Minor Children* (form FL-270)

   and

   d. ☑ (1) ☑ Completed and blank *Declaration Under Uniform Child Custody Jurisdiction and Enforcement Act (UCCJEA)* (form FL-105)

   (2) ☐ Completed and blank *Declaration of Disclosure* (form FL-140)

   (3) ☐ Completed and blank *Schedule of Assets and Debts* (form FL-142)

   (4) ☐ Completed and blank *Income and Expense Declaration* (form FL-150)

   (5) ☐ Completed and blank *Financial Statement (Simplified)* (form FL-155)

   (6) ☐ Completed and blank *Property Declaration* (form FL-160)

   (7) ☐ *Request for Order* (form FL-300), and blank *Responsive Declaration to Request for Order* (form FL-320)

   (8) ☑ Other *(specify)*:
   Declaration of Residence

2. Address where respondent was served:
   8675 Eighty-Sixth Street, Splittsville, CA 92395

3. I served the respondent by the following means *(check proper boxes)*:
   a. ☑ **Personal service.** I personally delivered the copies to the respondent (Code Civ. Proc., § 415.10)
   on *(date)*: February 13, 2021   at *(time)*: 7:51 p.m.
   b. ☐ **Substituted service.** I left the copies with or in the presence of *(name)*:
   who is *(specify title or relationship to respondent)*:

      (1) ☐ **(Business)** a person at least 18 years of age who was apparently in charge at the office or usual place of business of the respondent. I informed the person of the general nature of the papers.

      (2) ☐ **(Home)** a competent member of the household (at least 18 years of age) at the home of the respondent. I informed the person of the general nature of the papers.

   on *(date)*:   at *(time)*:

   I thereafter mailed additional copies (by first class, postage prepaid) to the respondent at the place where the copies were left (Code Civ. Proc., § 415.20b) on *(date)*:

   A **declaration of diligence** is attached, stating the actions taken to first attempt personal service.

   Page 1 of 2

FL-115

PETITIONER: Ima Dunn Hatchet	CASE NUMBER:
RESPONDENT: Barry D. Hatchet	XYZ123456

3. c. ☐ **Mail and acknowledgment service.** I mailed the copies to the respondent, addressed as shown in item 2, by first-class mail, postage prepaid, on *(date)*:　　　　　　　　　　　from *(city)*:

(1) ☐ with two copies of the *Notice and Acknowledgment of Receipt* (form FL-117) and a postage-paid return envelope addressed to me. **(Attach completed *Notice and Acknowledgment of Receipt* (form FL-117).)** (Code Civ. Proc., § 415.30.)

(2) ☐ to an address outside California (by registered or certified mail with return receipt requested). **(Attach signed return receipt or other evidence of actual delivery to the respondent.)** (Code Civ. Proc., §§ 415.40, 417.20.)

d. ☐ **Other** *(specify code section)*:

☐ Continued on Attachment 3d.

4. **Person who served papers**

Name: Al E. Gator, Process Server
Address: 555 Arty Fischel Road
　　　　　Splittsville, CA 92395

Telephone number:

This person is

a. ☐ exempt from registration under Business and Professions Code section 22350(b).
b. ☐ not a registered California process server.
c. ☑ a registered California process server: ☐ an employee or ☐ an independent contractor
　　(1) Registration no.: 123
　　(2) County: Riverside
d. ☐ The fee for service was *(specify)*: $ 65.00

5. ☑ I declare under penalty of perjury under the laws of the State of California that the foregoing is true and correct.

　　　　　　　　　　　　　　　　　　　　　–or–

6. ☐ I am a California sheriff, marshal, or constable, and I certify that the foregoing is true and correct.

Date: 03/20/2021

Al E. Gator
[NAME OF PERSON WHO SERVED PAPERS]

▶ *Al E. Gator*
(SIGNATURE OF PERSON WHO SERVED PAPERS)

FL-115 [Rev. January 1, 2021]

PROOF OF SERVICE OF SUMMONS
(Family Law—Uniform Parentage—Custody and Support)

Page 2 of 2

FL-120

PARTY WITHOUT ATTORNEY OR ATTORNEY	STATE BAR NUMBER	FOR COURT USE ONLY
NAME: Barry D. Hatchet		

FIRM NAME: In Pro Per
STREET ADDRESS: 8675 Eighty-Sixth Street
CITY: Splittsville   STATE: CA   ZIP CODE: 92395
TELEPHONE NO.: 951-555-1212   FAX NO.:
E-MAIL ADDRESS: SamPull@gmail.com
ATTORNEY FOR (name): Ima Dunn Hatchet

SUPERIOR COURT OF CALIFORNIA, COUNTY OF Riverside
STREET ADDRESS: 880 N. State Street
MAILING ADDRESS:
CITY AND ZIP CODE: Hemet 92543
BRANCH NAME: Hemet Courthouse

PETITIONER: Ima Dunn Hatchet
RESPONDENT: Barry D. Hatchet

RESPONSE ☑ **AND REQUEST FOR**	☐ **AMENDED**	CASE NUMBER: XYZ123456

☑ Dissolution (Divorce) of:	☑ Marriage	☐ Domestic Partnership
☐ Legal Separation of:	☐ Marriage	☐ Domestic Partnership
☐ Nullity of:	☐ Marriage	☐ Domestic Partnership

1. **LEGAL RELATIONSHIP** *(check all that apply):*
   a. ☑ We are married.
   b. ☐ We are domestic partners and our domestic partnership was established in California.
   c. ☐ We are domestic partners and our domestic partnership was NOT established in California.

2. **RESIDENCE REQUIREMENTS** *(check all that apply):*
   a. ☑ Petitioner ☑ Respondent has been a resident of this state for at least six months and of this county for at least three months immediately preceding the filing of this *Petition.* *(For a divorce, unless you are in the legal relationship described in 1b., at least one of you must comply with this requirement.)*
   b. ☐ Our domestic partnership was established in California. Neither of us has to be a resident or have a domicile in California to dissolve our partnership here.
   c. ☐ We are the same sex, were married in California, but currently live in a jurisdiction that does not recognize, and will not dissolve, our marriage. This *Petition* is filed in the county where we married.
   Petitioner lives in *(specify):*   Respondent lives in *(specify):*

3. **STATISTICAL FACTS**
   a. ☑ (1) Date of marriage *(specify):* 10/10/2000   (2) Date of separation *(specify):* 1/22/2021
      (3) Time from date of marriage to date of separation *(specify):* 20   Years 2   Months
   b. ☐ (1) Registration date of domestic partnership with the California Secretary of State or other state equivalent *(specify below):*
      (2) Date of separation *(specify):*
      (3) Time from date of registration of domestic partnership to date of separation *(specify):*   Years   Months

4. **MINOR CHILDREN**
   a. ☐ There are no minor children.
   b. ☑ The minor children are:

Child's name	Birthdate	Age
Kay Oss Hatchet	12/23/2017	3 yrs
Upton O'Goode Hatchet	03/02/2014	6 yrs

   (1) ☐ continued on Attachment 4b.   (2) ☐ a child who is not yet born.
   c. If any children were born before the marriage or domestic partnership, the court has the authority to determine those children to be children of the marriage or domestic partnership.
   d. If there are minor children of Petitioner and Respondent, a completed *Declaration Under Uniform Child Custody Jurisdiction and Enforcement Act (UCCJEA)* (form FL-105) must be attached.
   e. ☐ Petitioner and Respondent signed a voluntary declaration of parentage or paternity. *(Attach a copy if available.)*

Page 1 of 3

RESPONSE—MARRIAGE/DOMESTIC PARTNERSHIP
(Family Law)

Family Code, § 2020
www.courts.ca.gov

FL-120

PETITIONER: Ima Dunn Hatchet RESPONDENT: Barry D. Hatchet	CASE NUMBER: XYZ123456

Respondent requests that the court make the following orders:

5. **LEGAL GROUNDS** (Family Code sections 2200–2210; 2310–2312)
   a. ☐ **Respondent contends** that the parties never legally married or registered a domestic partnership.
   b. ☑ **Respondent denies** the grounds set forth in item 5 of the petition.
   c. ☑ **Respondent requests**
      (1) ☑ Divorce ☐ Legal separation of the marriage or domestic partnership based on
         (a) ☑ irreconcilable differences. (b) ☐ permanent legal incapacity to make decisions.
      (2) ☐ Nullity of void marriage or domestic partnership based on
         (a) ☐ incest. (b) ☐ bigamy.
      (3) ☐ Nullity of voidable marriage or domestic partnership based on
         (a) ☐ respondent's age at time of registration of domestic partnership or marriage. (d) ☐ fraud.
         (b) ☐ prior existing marriage or domestic partnership. (e) ☐ force.
         (c) ☐ unsound mind. (f) ☐ physical incapacity.

6. **CHILD CUSTODY AND VISITATION (PARENTING TIME)**

	Petitioner	Respondent	Joint	Other
a. Legal custody of children to	☐	☑	☐	☐
b. Physical custody of children to	☐	☑	☐	☐
c. Child visitation (parenting time) be granted to	☐	☐	☐	☐

   As requested in ☐ form FL-311 ☐ form FL-312 ☐ form FL-341(C)
   ☐ form FL-341(D) ☐ form FL-341(E) ☐ Attachment 6c(1)

7. **CHILD SUPPORT**
   a. If there are minor children born to or adopted by Petitioner and Respondent before or during this marriage or domestic partnership, the court will make orders for the support of the children upon request and submission of financial forms by the requesting party.
   b. An earnings assignment may be issued without further notice.
   c. Any party required to pay support must pay interest on overdue amounts at the "legal" rate, which is currently 10 percent.
   d. ☐ Other (specify):

8. **SPOUSAL OR DOMESTIC PARTNER SUPPORT**
   a. ☑ Spousal or domestic partner support payable to ☐ Petitioner ☑ Respondent
   b. ☑ Terminate (end) the court's ability to award support to ☑ Petitioner ☐ Respondent
   c. ☐ Reserve for future determination the issue of support payable to ☐ Petitioner ☐ Respondent
   d. ☐ Other (specify):

9. **SEPARATE PROPERTY**
   a. ☐ There are no such assets or debts that I know of to be confirmed by the court.
   b. ☑ Confirm as separate property the assets and debts in ☐ Property Declaration (form FL-160). ☐ Attachment 9b.
      ☑ the following list. Item Confirm to
      All acquisitions before marriage and post-separation and all gifts, and the balance of the assets and obligations, separate or otherwise, are unknown to Petitioner who will amend these pleadings once ascertained or according to proof at the time of Trial.

FL-120

| PETITIONER: Ima Dunn Hatchet | CASE NUMBER: |
| RESPONDENT: Barry D. Hatchet | XYZ123456 |

10. COMMUNITY AND QUASI-COMMUNITY PROPERTY

a. ☐ There are no such assets or debts that I know of to be divided by the court.

b. ☑ Determine rights to community and quasi-community assets and debts. All such assets and debts are listed
   ☐ in Property Declaration (form FL-160).   ☐ in Attachment 10b.
   ☑ as follows (specify):
   Real property; motor vehicles; furniture; furnishings and appliances; debts;
   retirement accounts; financial accounts; and the balance of the assets and obligations, community or
   otherwise, are unknown to Petitioner who will amend these pleadings once ascertained or according to
   proof at time of Trial

11. OTHER REQUESTS

a. ☑ Attorney's fees and costs payable by   ☑ Petitioner   ☐ Respondent

b. ☐ Respondent's former name be restored to (specify):

c. ☐ Other (specify):

☐ Continued on Attachment 11c.

I declare under penalty of perjury under the laws of the State of California that the foregoing is true and correct.

Date: 03/20/2021

Barry D. Hatchet   ▶ *Barry D. Hatchet*
(TYPE OR PRINT NAME)   (SIGNATURE OF RESPONDENT)

Date:

_____   ▶ _____
(TYPE OR PRINT NAME)   (SIGNATURE OF ATTORNEY FOR RESPONDENT)

FOR MORE INFORMATION: Read *Legal Steps for a Divorce or Legal Separation* (form FL-107-INFO) and visit "Families Change"
at *www.familieschange.ca.gov* — an online guide for parents and children going through divorce or separation.

NOTICE: You may redact (black out) social security numbers from any written material filed with the court in this case other than a
form used to collect child, spousal or partner support.

NOTICE—CANCELLATION OF RIGHTS: Dissolution or legal separation may automatically cancel the rights of a domestic partner
or spouse under the other domestic partner's or spouse's will, trust, retirement plan, power of attorney, pay-on-death bank account,
survivorship rights to any property owned in joint tenancy, and any other similar thing. It does not automatically cancel the right of a
domestic partner or spouse as beneficiary of the other partner's or spouse's life insurance policy. You should review these matters,
as well as any credit cards, other credit accounts, insurance polices, retirement plans, and credit reports, to determine whether they
should be changed or whether you should take any other actions. Some changes may require the agreement of your partner or
spouse or a court order.

The original response must be filed in the court with proof of service of a copy on Petitioner.

FL-120 [Rev. January 1, 2020]   **RESPONSE—MARRIAGE/DOMESTIC PARTNERSHIP**   Page 3 of 3
                                                    (Family Law)

FL-335

ATTORNEY OR PARTY WITHOUT ATTORNEY *(Name, State Bar number, and address):*	FOR COURT USE ONLY
Barry D. Hatchet — In Pro Per 8675 Eighty-Sixth Street Splitsville CA 92395 TELEPHONE NO: **951-555-1212** FAX NO. *(Optional):* E-MAIL ADDRESS *(Optional):* **SamPull@gmail.com** ATTORNEY FOR *(Name):* Ima Dunn Hatchet	

SUPERIOR COURT OF CALIFORNIA, COUNTY OF Riverside
STREET ADDRESS: **880 N. State Street**
MAILING ADDRESS:
CITY AND ZIP CODE: **Hemet 92543**
BRANCH NAME: **Hemet Courthouse**

PETITIONER/PLAINTIFF: **Ima Dunn Hatchet**	CASE NUMBER: **XYZ123456**
RESPONDENT/DEFENDANT: **Barry D. Hatchet**	*(If applicable, provide):*
OTHER PARENT/PARTY:	HEARING DATE:
PROOF OF SERVICE BY MAIL	HEARING TIME: DEPT.:

NOTICE: To serve temporary restraining orders you must use personal service (see form FL-330).

1. I am at least 18 years of age, not a party to this action, and I am a resident of or employed in the county where the mailing took place.

2. My residence or business address is:
   Justin Thyme
   777 Jack Pott Way
   Splittsville, CA   92395

3. I served a copy of the following documents *(specify):*
   Response-Marriage and Declaration Under Uniform Child Custody Jurisdiction Enforcement Act

   by enclosing them in an envelope AND
   a. ☐ **depositing** the sealed envelope with the United States Postal Service with the postage fully prepaid.
   b. ☑ **placing** the envelope for collection and mailing on the date and at the place shown in item 4 following our ordinary business practices. I am readily familiar with this business's practice for collecting and processing correspondence for mailing. On the same day that correspondence is placed for collection and mailing, it is deposited in the ordinary course of business with the United States Postal Service in a sealed envelope with postage fully prepaid.

4. The envelope was addressed and mailed as follows:
   a. Name of person served: Ima Dunn Hatchet
   b. Address: 1234 Rocky Road
      Splitsville CA 92395
   c. Date mailed: 3/11/2021
   d. Place of mailing *(city and state):*

5. ☐ I served a request to modify a child custody, visitation, or child support judgment or permanent order which included an address verification declaration. *(Declaration Regarding Address Verification—Postjudgment Request to Modify a Child Custody, Visitation, or Child Support Order* (form FL-334) may be used for this purpose.)

6. I declare under penalty of perjury under the laws of the State of California that the foregoing is true and correct.
   Date: 03/20/2021

   Justin Thyme

   Justin Thyme
   _____
   (TYPE OR PRINT NAME)

   ▶ *Justin Thyme*
   _____
   (SIGNATURE OF PERSON COMPLETING THIS FORM)

   Page 1 of 1

Form Approved for Optional Use Judicial Council of California FL-335 [Rev. January 1, 2012]	**PROOF OF SERVICE BY MAIL**	Code of Civil Procedure, §§ 1013, 1013a www.courts.ca.gov

FL-140

ATTORNEY OR PARTY WITHOUT ATTORNEY (Name, State Bar number, and address): Ima Dunn Hatchet In Pro Per 1234 Rocky Road Splitsville CA 92395 TELEPHONE NO.: 951-555-1212 FAX NO. : E-MAIL ADDRESS: SamPull@gmail.com ATTORNEY FOR (Name): Ima Dunn Hatchet	
SUPERIOR COURT OF CALIFORNIA, COUNTY OF Riverside STREET ADDRESS: 580 N. State Street MAILING ADDRESS: CITY AND ZIP CODE: Hemet 92543 BRANCH NAME: Hemet Courthouse	
PETITIONER: Ima Dunn Hatchet RESPONDENT: Barry D. Hatchet OTHER PARENT/PARTY:	

DECLARATION OF DISCLOSURE [✓] Petitioner's [✓] Preliminary [ ] Respondent's [ ] Final	CASE NUMBER: XYZ123456

DO NOT FILE DECLARATIONS OF DISCLOSURE OR FINANCIAL ATTACHMENTS WITH THE COURT

In a dissolution, legal separation, or nullity action, both a preliminary and a final declaration of disclosure must be served on the other party with certain exceptions. Neither disclosure is filed with the court. Instead, a declaration stating that service of disclosure documents was completed or waived must be filed with the court (see form FL-141).

* *In summary dissolution cases, each spouse or domestic partner must exchange preliminary disclosures as described in Summary Dissolution Information (form FL-810). Final disclosures are not required (see Family Code section 2109).*

* *In a default judgment case that is not a stipulated judgment or a judgment based on a marital settlement agreement, only the petitioner is required to complete and serve a preliminary declaration of disclosure. A final disclosure is not required of either party (see Family Code section 2110).*

* *Service of preliminary declarations of disclosure may not be waived by an agreement between the parties.*

* *Parties who agree to waive final declarations of disclosure must file their written agreement with the court (see form FL-144).*

The petitioner must serve a preliminary declaration of disclosure at the same time as the Petition or within 60 days of filing the Petition. The respondent must serve a preliminary declaration of disclosure at the same time as the Response or within 60 days of filing the Response. The time periods may be extended by written agreement of the parties or by court order (see Family Code section 2104(f)).

Attached are the following:

1. [✓] A completed *Schedule of Assets and Debts* (form FL-142) or [ ] A *Property Declaration* (form FL-160) for *(specify):*
   [ ] Community and Quasi-Community Property   [ ] Separate Property.

2. [✓] A completed *Income and Expense Declaration* (form FL-150).

3. [✓] All tax returns filed by the party in the two years before the date that the party served the disclosure documents.

4. [ ] A statement of all material facts and information regarding valuation of all assets that are community property or in which the community has an interest *(not a form)*.

5. [ ] A statement of all material facts and information regarding obligations for which the community is liable *(not a form)*.

6. [ ] An accurate and complete written disclosure of any investment opportunity, business opportunity, or other income-producing opportunity presented since the date of separation that results from any investment, significant business, or other income-producing opportunity from the date of marriage to the date of separation *(not a form)*.

I declare under penalty of perjury under the laws of the State of California that the foregoing is true and correct.

Date: 03/20/2021   *Ima Dunn Hatchet*

Ima Dunn Hatchet
,TYPE OR PRINT NAME)   SIGNATURE

Page 1 of 1

Form Adopted for Mandatory Use Judicial Council of California FL-140 [Rev. July 1, 2013]	**DECLARATION OF DISCLOSURE** **(Family Law)**	Family Code, §§ 2102, 2104, 2105, 2106, 2112 www.courts.ca.gov

FL-150

PARTY WITHOUT ATTORNEY OR ATTORNEY	STATE BAR NUMBER	FOR COURT USE ONLY
NAME: Ima Dunn Hatchet		
FIRM NAME: In Pro Per		
STREET ADDRESS: 1234 Rocky Road		
CITY: Splitsville STATE: CA ZIP CODE: 92395		
TELEPHONE NO.: 951-555-1212 FAX NO.:		
E MAIL ADDRESS: SamPull@gmail.com		
ATTORNEY FOR (name): Ima Dunn Hatchet		

SUPERIOR COURT OF CALIFORNIA, COUNTY OF Riverside
STREET ADDRESS: 880 N. State Street
MAILING ADDRESS:
CITY AND ZIP CODE: Hemet 92543
BRANCH NAME: Hemet Courthouse

PETITIONER: Ima Dunn Hatchet
RESPONDENT: Barry D. Hatchet
OTHER PARTY/PARENT/CLAIMANT:

INCOME AND EXPENSE DECLARATION	CASE NUMBER: D123456

1. **Employment** *(Give information on your current job or, if you're unemployed, your most recent job.)*

Attach copies of your pay stubs for last two months (black out Social Security numbers).

a. Employer: It's A Job
b. Employer's address: 777 Working Way
c. Employer's phone number: 888-555-7777
d. Occupation: Customer Service
e. Date job started: 2/12/2021
f. If unemployed, date job ended:
g. I work about 40 hours per week.
h. I get paid $ 15 gross (before taxes) [ ] per month [ ] per week [✔] per hour.

(If you have more than one job, attach an 8 1/2-by-11-inch sheet of paper and list the same information as above for your other jobs. Write "Question 1—Other Jobs" at the top.)

2. **Age and education**
   a. My age is *(specify):* 49
   b. I have completed high school or the equivalent: [✔] Yes [ ] No If no, highest grade completed *(specify):*
   c. Number of years of college completed *(specify):* [ ] Degree(s) obtained *(specify):*
   d. Number of years of graduate school completed *(specify):* [ ] Degree(s) obtained *(specify):*
   e. I have: [ ] professional/occupational license(s) *(specify):*
      [ ] vocational training *(specify):*

3. **Tax information**
   a. [✔] I last filed taxes for tax year *(specify year):* 2020
   b. My tax filing status is [ ] single [ ] head of household [ ] married, filing separately
      [ ] married, filing jointly with *(specify name):* Barry D. Hatchet
   c. I file state tax returns in [✔] California [ ] other *(specify state):*
   d. I claim the following number of exemptions (including myself) on my taxes *(specify):*

4. **Other party's income.** I estimate the gross monthly income (before taxes) of the other party in this case at *(specify):* $ 10,000/mo. This estimate is based on *(explain):* 2020 Income Tax Returns

(If you need more space to answer any questions on this form, attach an 8 1/2-by-11-inch sheet of paper and write the question number before your answer.) Number of pages attached: 4

I declare under penalty of perjury under the laws of the State of California that the information contained on all pages of this form and any attachments is true and correct.

Date: 03/20/2021

Ima Dunn Hatchet

Ima Dunn Hatchet
_____
(TYPE OR PRINT NAME)

▶ *Ima Dunn Hatchet*
_____
(SIGNATURE OF DECLARANT)

Page 1 of 4

Form Adopted for Mandatory Use
Judicial Council of California
FL-150 [Rev. January 1, 2019]

INCOME AND EXPENSE DECLARATION

Family Code, §§ 2030–2032, 2100–2113,
3552, 3620–3634, 4050–4076, 4300–4339
www.courts.ca.gov

FL-150

	CASE NUMBER:
PETITIONER: **Ima Dunn Hatchet**	D123456
RESPONDENT: **Barry D. Hatchet**	
OTHER PARTY/PARENT/CLAIMANT:	

Attach copies of your pay stubs for the last two months and proof of any other income. Take a copy of your latest federal tax return to the court hearing. *(Black out your Social Security number on the pay stub and tax return.)*

5. **Income** *(For average monthly, add up all the income you received in each category in the last 12 months and divide the total by 12.)*

		Last month	Average monthly
a.	Salary or wages (gross, before taxes)..	$ 4000	4000
b.	Overtime (gross, before taxes)...	$	
c.	Commissions or bonuses..	$	
d.	Public assistance (for example: TANF, SSI, GA/GR) ☐ currently receiving	$	
e.	Spousal support ☐ from this marriage ☐ from a different marriage ☐ federally taxable*	$	
f.	Partner support ☐ from this domestic partnership ☐ from a different domestic partnership	$	
g.	Pension/retirement fund payments..	$	
h.	Social Security retirement (not SSI)..	$	
i.	Disability: ☐ Social Security (not SSI) ☐ State disability (SDI) ☐ Private insurance	$	
j.	Unemployment compensation...	$	
k.	Workers' compensation..	$	
l.	Other (military allowances, royalty payments) *(specify):*	$	

6. **Investment income** *(Attach a schedule showing gross receipts less cash expenses for each piece of property.)*

a.	Dividends/interest...	$
b.	Rental property income...	$
c.	Trust income..	$
d.	Other *(specify):*	$

7. **Income from self-employment, after business expenses for all businesses**................ $ _____

I am the ☐ owner/sole proprietor ☐ business partner ☐ other *(specify):*
Number of years in this business *(specify):*
Name of business *(specify):*
Type of business *(specify):*

Attach a profit and loss statement for the last two years or a Schedule C from your last federal tax return. Black out your Social Security number. If you have more than one business, provide the information above for each of your businesses.

8. ☐ **Additional income.** I received one-time money (lottery winnings, inheritance, etc.) in the last 12 months *(specify source and amount):*

9. ☐ **Change in income.** My financial situation has changed significantly over the last 12 months because *(specify):*

10. **Deductions** — Last month

a.	Required union dues..	$
b.	Required retirement payments (not Social Security, FICA, 401(k), or IRA).....................	$
c.	Medical, hospital, dental, and other health insurance premiums *(total monthly amount)*....	$
d.	Child support that I pay for children from other relationships	$
e.	Spousal support that I pay by court order from a different marriage ☐ federally tax deductible*....	$
f.	Partner support that I pay by court order from a different domestic partnership.	$
g.	Necessary job-related expenses not reimbursed by my employer *(attach explanation labeled "Question 10g")*........	$

11. **Assets** — Total

a.	Cash and checking accounts, savings, credit union, money market, and other deposit accounts..........	$ 5,00
b.	Stocks, bonds, and other assets I could easily sell...	$ 5000
c.	All other property, ☑ real and ☑ personal *(estimate fair market value minus the debts you owe)*.....	$ 550000

* Check the box if the spousal support order or judgment was executed by the parties and the court before January 1, 2019, or if a court-ordered change maintains the spousal support payments as taxable income to the recipient and tax deductible to the payor.

FL-150

PETITIONER: Ima Dunn Hatchet	CASE NUMBER:
RESPONDENT: Barry D. Hatchet	D123456
OTHER PARTY/PARENT/CLAIMANT:	

12. The following people live with me:

Name	Age	How the person is related to me (ex: son)	That person's gross monthly income	Pays some of the household expenses?
a. Kay Oss Hatchet	3	Daughter	0.00	☐ Yes ☑ No
b. Upton O'Goode Hatchet	6	Son	0.00	☐ Yes ☑ No
c. Herbie Dunn	75	Father	10,000	☑ Yes ☐ No
d.				☐ Yes ☐ No
e.				☐ Yes ☐ No

13. Average monthly expenses ☑ Estimated expenses ☑ Actual expenses ☑ Proposed needs

a. Home:

   (1) ☑ Rent or ☐ mortgage......... $ 2500

   If mortgage:

    (a) average principal: $ _____

    (b) average interest: $ _____

   (2) Real property taxes....................... $ _____

   (3) Homeowner's or renter's insurance (if not included above)............................ $ _____

   (4) Maintenance and repair.................. $ _____

b. Health-care costs not paid by insurance. ...... $ _____

c. Child care... $ 500

d. Groceries and household supplies................ $ 1000

e. Eating out.. $ _____

f. Utilities (gas, electric, water, trash)............ $ 600

g. Telephone, cell phone, and e-mail............... $ 150

h. Laundry and cleaning.................................. $ _____

i. Clothes.. $ _____

j. Education.. $ _____

k. Entertainment, gifts, and vacation................ $ _____

l. Auto expenses and transportation (insurance, gas, repairs, bus, etc.)................ $ 150

m. Insurance (life, accident, etc.; do not include auto, home, or health insurance).................. $ _____

n. Savings and investments............................ $ _____

o. Charitable contributions.............................. $ _____

p. Monthly payments listed in item 14 (itemize below in 14 and insert total here)..... $ 25.00

q. Other (specify): $ _____

r. **TOTAL EXPENSES** (a–q) (do not add in the amounts in a(1)(a) and (b)) **$ 4,925.00**

s. **Amount of expenses paid by others** **$ 1,500.00**

14 Installment payments and debts not listed above

Paid to	For	Amount	Balance	Date of last payment
Visa	Credit Card	$25	$8000	current
		$	$	
		$	$	
		$	$	
		$	$	

15. Attorney fees (This information is required if either party is requesting attorney fees):

a. To date, I have paid my attorney this amount for fees and costs (specify): $

b. The source of this money was (specify):

c. I still owe the following fees and costs to my attorney (specify total owed): $

d. My attorney's hourly rate is (specify):

I confirm this fee arrangement.

Date:

Ima Dunn Hatchet
_____
(TYPE OR PRINT NAME)

▶

(SIGNATURE OF DECLARANT)

FL-150

	CASE NUMBER:
PETITIONER: Ima Dunn Hatchet	D123456
RESPONDENT: Barry D. Hatchet	
OTHER PARTY/PARENT/CLAIMANT:	

CHILD SUPPORT INFORMATION
(NOTE: Fill out this page only if your case involves child support.)

16. **Number of children**
   a. I have *(specify number):* 2   children under the age of 18 with the other parent in this case.
   b. The children spend 70   percent of their time with me and 30   percent of their time with the other parent.
   (If you're not sure about percentage or it has not been agreed on, please describe your parenting schedule here.)
   Respondent has the children in his care, custody and control. every other weekend 1 overnight per weeks.

17. **Children's health-care expenses**
   a. [ ] I do   [✔] I do not   have health insurance available to me for the children through my job.
   b. Name of insurance company:
   c. Address of insurance company:

   d. The monthly cost for the **children's** health insurance is or would be *(specify):* $
   (Do not include the amount your employer pays.)

18. **Additional expense for the children in this case**   Amount per month
   a. Childcare so I can work or get job training... $
   b. Children's health care not covered by insurance................................... $
   c. Travel expenses for visitation.. $
   d. Children's educational or other special needs *(specify below):*.............. $

19. **Special hardships.** I ask the court to consider the following special financial circumstances
   (attach documentation of any item listed here, including court orders):

	Amount per month	For how many months?
a. Extraordinary health expenses not included in 18b....................... $		
b. Major losses not covered by insurance *(examples: fire, theft, other insured loss)*.. $		
c. (1) Expenses for my minor children who are from other relationships and are living with me... $		

   (2) Names and ages of those children *(specify):*

   (3) Child support I receive for those children................................ $
   The expenses listed in a, b, and c create an extreme financial hardship because *(explain):*

20. **Other information I want the court to know concerning support in my case** *(specify):*

    INCOME AND EXPENSE DECLARATION

THIS FORM SHOULD NOT BE FILED WITH THE COURT

FL-142

ATTORNEY OR PARTY WITHOUT ATTORNEY *(Name and Address)*: Ima Dunn Hatchet In Pro Per 1234 Rocky Road Splitsville CA 92395 ATTORNEY FOR *(Name)*: Ima Dunn Hatchet	TELEPHONE NO.: 951-555-1212

SUPERIOR COURT OF CALIFORNIA, COUNTY OF Riverside

PETITIONER: Ima Dunn Hatchet

RESPONDENT: Barry D. Hatchet

SCHEDULE OF ASSETS AND DEBTS ☑ Petitioner's ☐ Respondent's	CASE NUMBER: XYZ123456

— INSTRUCTIONS —

List all your known community and separate assets or debts. Include assets even if they are in the possession of another person, including your spouse. If you contend an asset or debt is separate, put P (for Petitioner) or R (for Respondent) in the first column (separate property) to indicate to whom you contend it belongs.

All values should be as of the date of signing the declaration unless you specify a different valuation date with the description. For additional space, use a continuation sheet numbered to show which item is being continued.

ITEM NO. ASSETS DESCRIPTION	SEP. PROP	DATE ACQUIRED	CURRENT GROSS FAIR MARKET VALUE	AMOUNT OF MONEY OWED OR ENCUMBRANCE
1. REAL ESTATE *(Give street addresses and attach copies of deeds with legal descriptions and latest lender's statement.)* 1234 Rocky Road, Splitsville, CA 92395		Dur. Mar.	$ 450,000	$ 260,000
2. HOUSEHOLD FURNITURE, FURNISHINGS, APPLIANCES *(Identify.)* Misc. Household, furniture, furnishings & Applicances		Dur. Mar.	5000	
3. JEWELRY, ANTIQUES, ART, COIN COLLECTIONS, etc. *(Identify.)* Ima's Wedding Ring (Gift) Barry's Wedding Ring (Gift)	P R	Dur. Mar. Dur. Mar.	2500 500	

Form Approved for Optional Use
Judicial Council of California
FL-142 [Rev. January 1, 2005]

SCHEDULE OF ASSETS AND DEBTS
(Family Law)

Code of Civil Procedure, §§ 2030(c), 2033.5
www.courtinfo.ca.gov

ITEM NO.	ASSETS DESCRIPTION	SEP. PROP	DATE ACQUIRED	CURRENT GROSS FAIR MARKET VALUE	AMOUNT OF MONEY OWED OR ENCUMBRANCE
				$	$
4. VEHICLES, BOATS, TRAILERS (Describe and attach copy of title document.) 2020 Chevy Suburban 2018 Subaru Forester			Dur. Mar Dur. Mar.	20000 10000	16000 4000
5. SAVINGS ACCOUNTS (Account name, account number, bank, and branch. Attach copy of latest statement.) Acme Bank, Checking Account ending 1234			Dur. Mar.	350	0.00
6. CHECKING ACCOUNTS (Account name and number, bank, and branch. Attach copy of latest statement.) Acme Bank, Savings Account ending 5678			Dur. Mar.	10000	
7. CREDIT UNION, OTHER DEPOSIT ACCOUNTS (Account name and number, bank, and branch. Attach copy of latest statement.)					
8. CASH (Give location.) Cash on Hand in Safe			Dur. Mar.	2000	
9. TAX REFUND 2020 Income Tax Refund			Dur. Mar.	1500	
10. LIFE INSURANCE WITH CASH SURRENDER OR LOAN VALUE (Attach copy of declaration page for each policy.)					

FL-142 [Rev. January 1, 2005]

SCHEDULE OF ASSETS AND DEBTS
(Family Law)

ITEM NO.	ASSETS DESCRIPTION	SEP. PROP	DATE ACQUIRED	CURRENT GROSS FAIR MARKET VALUE	AMOUNT OF MONEY OWED OR ENCUMBRANCE
11.	STOCKS, BONDS, SECURED NOTES. MUTUAL FUNDS *(Give certificate number and attach copy of the certificate or copy of latest statement.)* 200 Shares Exxon/Moble 350 Shares Pepsi Co.		Dur. Mar. Dur. Mar.	$ 5700 2600	$
12.	RETIREMENT AND PENSIONS *(Attach copy of latest summary plan documents and latest benefit statement.)* Barry's 401(K) with American Retirement Fund Ima's IRA		Dur. Mar. Dur. Mar.	151000 2500	
13.	PROFIT · SHARING, ANNUITIES. IRAS, DEFERRED COMPENSATION *(Attach copy of latest statement.)*				
14.	ACCOUNTS RECEIVABLE AND UNSECURED NOTES *(Attach copy of each.)*				
15.	PARTNERSHIPS AND OTHER BUSINESS INTERESTS *(Attach copy of most current K-1 form and Schedule C.)*				
16.	OTHER ASSETS				
17.	TOTAL ASSETS FROM CONTINUATION SHEET				
18.	TOTAL ASSETS			$ 663,650.00	$ 280,000.00

SCHEDULE OF ASSETS AND DEBTS
(Family Law)

ITEM NO.	DEBTS—SHOW TO WHOM OWED	SEP. PROP.	TOTAL OWING	DATE INCURRED
19.	STUDENT LOANS *(Give details.)*		$	
20.	TAXES *(Give details.)*			
21.	SUPPORT ARREARAGES *(Attach copies of orders and statements.)*			
22.	LOANS—UNSECURED *(Give bank name and loan number and attach copy of latest statement.)*			
23.	CREDIT CARDS *(Give creditor's name and address and the account number. Attach copy of latest statement.)* Visa Credit Card in Ima's Name Master Card Credit Card in Barry's Name American Express in Both Names		7500 10350 6100	Dur. Mar. Dur. Mar. Dur. Mar.
24.	OTHER DEBTS *(Specify.):* Loan from Aunt Mary		3500	Dur. Mar.
25.	TOTAL DEBTS FROM CONTINUATION SHEET			
26.	TOTAL DEBTS		$ 27,450.00	

27. ☐ *(Specify number):* _____ pages are attached as continuation sheets.

I declare under penalty of perjury under the laws of the State of California that the foregoing is true and correct.

Date: 03/20/2021

Ima Dunn Hatchet

Ima Dunn Hatchet
    (TYPE OR PRINT NAME)

(SIGNATURE OF DECLARANT)

SCHEDULE OF ASSETS AND DEBTS
(Family Law)

FL-141

ATTORNEY OR PARTY WITHOUT ATTORNEY *(Name, State Bar number, and address):* Ima Dunn Hatchet In Pro Per 1234 Rocky Road Splitsville CA 92395	
TELEPHONE NO.: 951-555-1212 FAX NO.: E-MAIL ADDRESS: SamPull@gmail.com ATTORNEY FOR *(Name):* Ima Dunn Hatchet	

SUPERIOR COURT OF CALIFORNIA, COUNTY OF Riverside
STREET ADDRESS: 880 N. State Street
MAILING ADDRESS:
CITY AND ZIP CODE: Hemet 92543
BRANCH NAME: Hemet Courthouse

PETITIONER: Ima Dunn Hatchet
RESPONDENT: Barry D. Hatchet
OTHER PARENT/PARTY:

DECLARATION REGARDING SERVICE OF DECLARATION OF DISCLOSURE AND INCOME AND EXPENSE DECLARATION [✓] Petitioner's [✓] Preliminary [ ] Respondent's [ ] Final	CASE NUMBER: XYZ123456

1. I am the [ ] attorney for [✓] petitioner [ ] respondent in this matter.

2. [✓] Petitioner's [ ] Respondent's *Preliminary Declaration of Disclosure* (form FL-140), current* *Income and Expense Declaration* (form FL-150), completed *Schedule of Assets and Debts* (form FL-142) or *Community and Separate Property Declarations* (form FL-160) with appropriate attachments, all tax returns filed by the party in the two years before service of the preliminary disclosures, and all other required information under Family Code section 2104 were served on:

   [✓] the other party [ ] the other party's attorney by [ ] personal service [✓] mail
   [ ] Other *(specify):*
   on *(date):* 3/15/2021

3. [ ] Petitioner's [ ] Respondent's *Final Declaration of Disclosure* (form FL-140), current* *Income and Expense Declaration* (form FL-150), completed *Schedule of Assets and Debts* (form FL-142) or *Community or Separate Property Declarations* (form FL-160) with attachments, and the material facts and information required by Family Code section 2105 were served on:

   [ ] the other party [ ] other party's attorney by [ ] personal service [ ] mail
   [ ] Other *(specify):*
   on *(date):*

4. [ ] Service of [ ] Petitioner's [ ] Respondent's [ ] preliminary [ ] final declaration of disclosure current income and expense declaration has been waived as follows:

   a. [ ] The parties agreed to waive final declaration of disclosure requirements under Family Code section 2105(d.)
   (Form FL-144 may be used for this purpose.) The waiver [ ] was filed on *(date):*
   [ ] is being filed at the same time as this form.

   b. [ ] The party has failed to comply with disclosure requirements, and the court has granted the request for voluntary waiver of receipt under Family Code section 2107 on *(date):*

   c. [ ] This is a default proceeding that does not include a stipulated judgment or settlement agreement. Petitioner waives final disclosure requirements under Family Code section 2110.

*Current is defined as completed within the past three months providing no facts have changed. (Cal. Rules of Court, rule 5.260.)

I declare under penalty of perjury under the laws of the State of California that the foregoing is true and correct:

Date: 03/20/2021

Ima Dunn Hatchet   *Ima Dunn Hatchet*
(TYPE OR PRINT NAME)   SIGNATURE

NOTE: File this document with the court.
Do not file a copy of the Preliminary or Final Declaration of Disclosure or any attachments to either declaration of disclosure with this document.

Page 1 of 1

Form Adopted for Mandatory Use
Judicial Council of California
FL-141 (Rev. July 1, 2013)

DECLARATION REGARDING SERVICE OF DECLARATION OF
DISCLOSURE AND INCOME AND EXPENSE DECLARATION
(Family Law)

Family Code, §§ 2102, 2104,
2105, 2106, 2112
www.courts.ca.gov

FL-145

ATTORNEY OR PARTY WITHOUT ATTORNEY *(Name, State Bar number, and address)*: Ima Dunn Hatchet In Pro Per 1234 Rocky Road Splitsville CA 92395	TELEPHONE NO. 951-555-1212

ATTORNEY FOR *(Name)*: Ima Dunn Hatchet

SUPERIOR COURT OF CALIFORNIA, COUNTY OF Riverside

SHORT TITLE:
In Re Marriage of Hatchet

FORM INTERROGATORIES–FAMILY LAW	CASE NUMBER:
Asking Party: Ima Dunn Hatchet	XYZ 123456
Answering Party: Barry D. Hatchet	
Set No.: ONE	

Sec. 1. Instructions to Both Parties

The interrogatories on page 2 of this form are intended to provide for the exchange of relevant information without unreasonable expense to the answering party. They do not change existing law relating to interrogatories, nor do they affect the answering party's right to assert any privilege or make any objection. **Privileges must be asserted.**

Sec. 2. Definitions

Words in **boldface** in these interrogatories are defined as follows:

(a) **Person** includes a natural person; a partnership; any kind of business, legal, or public entity; and its agents or employees.

(b) **Document** means all written, recorded, or graphic materials, however stored, produced, or reproduced.

(c) **Asset** or **property** includes any interest in real estate or personal property. It includes any interest in a pension, profit-sharing, or retirement plan.

(d) **Debt** means any obligation, including debts paid since the date of separation.

(e) **Support** means any benefit or economic contribution to the living expenses of another person, including gifts.

(f) If asked to **identify a person**, give the person's name, last known residence and business addresses, telephone numbers, and company affiliation at the date of the transaction referred to.

(g) If asked to **identify a document**, attach a copy of the document unless you explain why not. If you do not attach the copy, describe the document, including its date and nature, and give the name, address, telephone number, and occupation of the person who has the document.

Sec. 3. Instructions to the Asking Party

Check the box next to each interrogatory you want the answering party to answer.

Sec. 4. Instructions to the Answering Party

You must answer these interrogatories under oath within 30 days, in accordance with Code of Civil Procedure section 2030.260.

You must furnish all information you have or can reasonably find out, including all information (not privileged) from your attorneys or under your control. If you don't know, say so.

If an interrogatory is answered by referring to a document, the document must be attached as an exhibit to the response and referred to in the response. If the document has more than one page, refer to the page and section where the answer can be found.

If a document to be attached to the response may also be attached to the *Schedule of Assets and Debts* (form FL-142), the document should be attached only to the response, and the form should refer to the response.

If an interrogatory cannot be answered completely, answer as much as you can, state the reason you cannot answer the rest, and state any information you have about the unanswered portion.

Sec. 5. Oath

Your answers to these interrogatories must be under oath, dated, and signed. Use the following statement **at the end of your answers:**

I declare under penalty of perjury under the laws of the State of California that the foregoing answers are true and correct.

03/20/2021   *Barry D. Hatchet*

_____   ▶ _____
        (DATE)   (SIGNATURE)

Page 1 of 2

Form Approved for Optional Use
Judicial Council of California
FL-145 [Rev. January 1, 2006]

FORM INTERROGATORIES–FAMILY LAW

Code of Civil Procedure,
§§ 2030.010–2030.410, 2033.710
www.courtinfo.ca.gov

1. **Personal history.** State your full name, current residence address and work address, social security number, any other names you have used, and the dates between which you used each name.

2. **Agreements.** Are there any agreements between you and your spouse or domestic partner, made before or during your marriage or domestic partnership or after your separation, that affect the disposition of **assets, debts,** or **support** in this proceeding? If your answer is yes, for each agreement state the date made and whether it was written or oral, and attach a copy of the agreement or describe its contents.

3. **Legal actions.** Are you a party or do you anticipate being a party to any legal or administrative proceeding other than this action? If your answer is yes, state your role and the name, jurisdiction, case number, and a brief description of each proceeding

4. **Persons sharing residence.** State the name, age, and relationship to you of each **person** at your present address.

5. **Support provided others.** State the name, age, address, and relationship to you of each **person** for whom you have provided **support** during the past 12 months and the amount provided per month for each.

6. **Support received for others.** State the name, age, address, and relationship to you of each **person** for whom you have received **support** during the past 12 months and the amount received per month for each.

7. **Current income.** List all income you received during the past 12 months, its source, the basis for its computation, and the total amount received from each. Attach your last three paycheck stubs

8. **Other income.** During the past three years, have you received cash or other property from any source not identified in item 7? If so, list the source, the date, and the nature and value of the property.

9. **Tax returns.** Attach copies of all tax returns and tax schedules filed by or for you in any jurisdiction for the past three calendar years.

10. **Schedule of assets and debts.** Complete the *Schedule of Assets and Debts* (form FL-142) served with these interrogatories.

11. **Separate property contentions.** State the facts that support your contention that an asset or debt is separate property.

12. **Property valuations.** During the past 12 months, have you received written offers to purchase or had written appraisals of any of the assets listed on your completed *Schedule of Assets and Debts*? If your answer is yes, **identify the document.**

13. **Property held by others.** Is there any **property** held by any third party in which you have any interest or over which you have any control? If your answer is yes, indicate whether the property is shown on the *Schedule of Assets and Debts* completed by you. If it is not, describe and identify each such asset, state its present value and the basis for your valuation, and **identify the person** holding the asset.

14. **Retirement and other benefits.** Do you have an interest in any disability, retirement, profit-sharing, or deferred compensation plan? If your answer is yes, **identify** each plan and provide the name, address, and telephone number of the administrator and custodian of records.

15. **Claims of reimbursement.** Do you claim the legal right to be reimbursed for any expenditures of your separate or community property? If your answer is yes, state all supporting facts.

16. **Credits.** Have you claimed reimbursement credits for payments of community debts since the date of separation? If your answer is yes, **identify** the source of payment, the creditor, the date paid, and the amount paid. State whether you have added to the debt since the separation.

17. **Insurance.** Identify each health, life, automobile, and disability insurance policy or plan that you now own or that covers you, your children, or your assets. State the policy type, policy number, and name of the company. **Identify** the agent and give the address.

18. **Health.** Is there any physical or emotional condition that limits your ability to work? If your answer is yes, state each fact on which you base your answer.

19. **Children's needs.** Do you contend that any of your children have any special needs? If so, identify the child with the need, the reason for the need, its cost, and its expected duration.

20. **Attorney fees.** State the total amount of attorney fees and costs incurred by you in this proceeding, the amount paid, and the source of the money paid. Describe the billing arrangements.

21. **Gifts.** List any gifts you have made without the consent of your spouse or domestic partner in the past 24 months, their values, and the recipients.

FORM INTERROGATORIES–FAMILY LAW

FL-144

ATTORNEY OR PARTY WITHOUT ATTORNEY *(Name, State Bar number, and address):*	FOR COURT USE ONLY
Ima Dunn Hatchet In Pro Per 1234 Rocky Road Splitsville CA 92395 TELEPHONE NO.: 951-555-1212 FAX NO. *(Optional):* E-MAIL ADDRESS *(Optional):* SamPull@gmail.com ATTORNEY FOR *(Name):* Ima Dunn Hatchet	

SUPERIOR COURT OF CALIFORNIA, COUNTY OF Riverside	
STREET ADDRESS: 880 N. State Street	
MAILING ADDRESS:	
CITY AND ZIP CODE: Hemet 92543	
BRANCH NAME: Hemet Courthouse	

PLAINTIFF/ PETITIONER: Ima Dunn Hatchet	
DEFENDANT/ RESPONDENT: Barry D. Hatchet	
OTHER:	

	CASE NUMBER:
STIPULATION AND WAIVER OF FINAL DECLARATION OF DISCLOSURE	XYZ 123456

1. Under Family Code section 2105(d), the parties agree to waive the requirements of Family Code section 2105(a) concerning the final declaration of disclosure.

2. The parties agree as follows:

   a. We have complied with Family Code section 2104, and the preliminary declarations of disclosure have been completed and exchanged.

   b. We have completed and exchanged a current *Income and Expense Declaration* (form FL-150) that includes all material facts and information on each party's earnings, accumulations, and expenses.

   c. We have fully complied with Family Law section 2102 and have fully augmented the preliminary declarations of disclosure, including disclosure of all material facts and information on

      (1) the characterization of all assets and liabilities,

      (2) the valuation of all assets that are community property or in which the community has an interest, and

      (3) the amounts of all community debts and obligations.

   d. Each of the parties enters into this waiver knowingly, intelligently, and voluntarily.

   e. Each party understands that this waiver does not limit the legal disclosure obligations of the parties but rather is a statement under penalty of perjury that those obligations have been fulfilled.

   f. The parties also understand that if they do not comply with these obligations, the court will set aside the judgment.

The petitioner and respondent declare under penalty of perjury under the laws of the State of California that the foregoing is true and correct.

Date: 03/20/2021

Ima Dunn Hatchet

Ima Dunn Hatchet
(TYPE OR PRINT NAME)

(SIGNATURE OF PETITIONER)

Barry D. Hatchet

Barry D. Hatchet
(TYPE OR PRINT NAME)

(SIGNATURE OF RESPONDENT)

Page 1 of 1

Form Approved for Optional Use
Judicial Council of California
FL-144 [Rev. January 1, 2007]

STIPULATION AND WAIVER OF FINAL
DECLARATION OF DISCLOSURE

Family Code, §§ 2102, 2104, 2105(d)
www.courtinfo.ca.gov

FL-130

PARTY WITHOUT ATTORNEY *or* ATTORNEY STATE BAR NO.: NAME: **Ima Dunn Hatchet** FIRM NAME: **In Pro Per** STREET ADDRESS: **1234 Rocky Road** CITY: **Splitsville** STATE: **CA** ZIP CODE: **92395** TELEPHONE NO.: **951-555-1212** FAX NO.: E-MAIL ADDRESS: **SamPull@gmail.com** ATTORNEY FOR (name): **Ima Dunn Hatchet**	FOR COURT USE ONLY
SUPERIOR COURT OF CALIFORNIA, COUNTY OF **Riverside** STREET ADDRESS: **880 N. State Street** MAILING ADDRESS: CITY AND ZIP CODE: **Hemet 92543** BRANCH NAME: **Hemet Courthouse** PETITIONER: **Ima Dunn Hatchet** RESPONDENT: **Barry D. Hatchet**	
APPEARANCE, STIPULATIONS, AND WAIVERS	CASE NUMBER: **XYZ 123456**

1. **Appearance by respondent** *(you must choose one)*:

   a. ☐ By filing this form, I make a general appearance.

   b. ☑ I have previously made a general appearance.

   c. ☐ I am a member of the military services of the United States of America. I have completed and attached to this form *Declaration and Conditional Waiver of Rights Under the Servicemembers Civil Relief Act of 2003* (form FL-130(A)).

2. **Agreements, stipulations, and waivers** *(choose all that apply)*:

   a. ☑ The parties agree that this cause may be decided as an uncontested matter.

   b. ☑ The parties waive their rights to notice of trial, a statement of decision, a motion for new trial, and the right to appeal.

   c. ☑ This matter may be decided by a commissioner sitting as a temporary judge.

   d. ☑ The parties have a written agreement that will be submitted to the court, or a stipulation for judgment will be submitted to the court and attached to *Judgment (Family Law)* (form FL-180).

   e. ☐ None of these agreements or waivers will apply unless the court approves the stipulation for judgment or incorporates the written settlement agreement into the judgment.

   f. ☐ This is a parentage case, and both parties have signed an *Advisement and Waiver of Rights Re: Determination of Parental Relationship* (form FL-235) or its equivalent.

3. **Other** *(specify)*:

03/20/2021

Date:

Ima Dunn Hatchet
_____
03/20/2021 (TYPE OR PRINT NAME)
Date:

Barry D. Hatchet
_____
(TYPE OR PRINT NAME)
Date:

_____
(TYPE OR PRINT NAME)
Date:

_____
(TYPE OR PRINT NAME)

Ima Dunn Hatchet
▶ _____
(SIGNATURE OF PETITIONER)

Barry D. Hatchet
▶ _____
(SIGNATURE OF RESPONDENT)

▶ _____
(SIGNATURE OF ATTORNEY FOR PETITIONER)

▶ _____
(SIGNATURE OF ATTORNEY FOR RESPONDENT)

Page 1 of 1

Form Approved for Optional Use
Judicial Council of California
FL-130 [Rev. January 1, 2021]

APPEARANCE, STIPULATIONS, AND WAIVERS
(Family Law—Uniform Parentage—Custody and Support)

Government Code, § 70673
www.courts.ca.gov

FL-190

ATTORNEY OR PARTY WITHOUT ATTORNEY *(Name, State Bar number, and address)*:	FOR COURT USE ONLY
Ima Dunn Hatchet In Pro Per 1234 Rocky Road Splitsville CA 92395 TELEPHONE NO.: 951-555-1212 FAX NO. *(Optional)*: E-MAIL ADDRESS *(Optional)*: SamPull@gmail.com ATTORNEY FOR *(Name)*: Ima Dunn Hatchet	

SUPERIOR COURT OF CALIFORNIA, COUNTY OF Riverside
STREET ADDRESS: 880 N. State Street
MAILING ADDRESS:
CITY AND ZIP CODE: Hemet 92543
BRANCH NAME: Hemet Courthouse

PETITIONER: Ima Dunn Hatchet

RESPONDENT: Barry D. Hatchet

NOTICE OF ENTRY OF JUDGMENT	CASE NUMBER: XYZ 123456

You are notified that the following judgment was entered on *(date)*:

1. ☑ Dissolution
2. ☐ Dissolution—status only
3. ☐ Dissolution—reserving jurisdiction over termination of marital status or domestic partnership
4. ☐ Legal separation
5. ☐ Nullity
6. ☐ Parent-child relationship
7. ☐ Judgment on reserved issues
8. ☐ Other *(specify)*:

Date: 03/20/2021

Ima Dunn Hatchet

Clerk, by _____, Deputy

—NOTICE TO ATTORNEY OF RECORD OR PARTY WITHOUT ATTORNEY—

Under the provisions of Code of Civil Procedure section 1952, if no appeal is filed the court may order the exhibits destroyed or otherwise disposed of after 60 days from the expiration of the appeal time.

STATEMENT IN THIS BOX APPLIES ONLY TO JUDGMENT OF DISSOLUTION
Effective date of termination of marital or domestic partnership status *(specify)*:
WARNING: Neither party may remarry or enter into a new domestic partnership until the effective date of the termination of marital or domestic partnership status, as shown in this box.

CLERK'S CERTIFICATE OF MAILING

I certify that I am not a party to this cause and that a true copy of the *Notice of Entry of Judgment* was mailed first class, postage fully prepaid, in a sealed envelope addressed as shown below, and that the notice was mailed

at *(place)*: _____, California,   on *(date)*: _____

Date: _____

Clerk, by _____, Deputy

--- Name and address of petitioner or petitioner's attorney ---
Ima Dunn Hatchet
1234 Rocky Road
Splittsville, CA 92395

--- Name and address of respondent or respondent's attorney ---
Barry D. Hatchet
8675 Eighty-Sixth Street
Splittsville, CA 92395

Page 1 of 1

Form Adopted for Mandatory Use
Judicial Council of California
FL-190 [Rev. January 1, 2005]

NOTICE OF ENTRY OF JUDGMENT
(Family Law—Uniform Parentage—Custody and Support)

Family Code, §§ 2328, 2626, 7637
www.courtinfo.ca.gov

FL-170

PARTY WITHOUT ATTORNEY OR ATTORNEY:	STATE BAR NUMBER:	FOR COURT USE ONLY
NAME: **Ima Dunn Hatchet**		
FIRM NAME: **In Pro Per**		
STREET ADDRESS: **1234 Rocky Road**		
CITY: **Splitsville** STATE: **CA** ZIP CODE: **92395**		
TELEPHONE NO.: **951-555-1212** FAX NO.:		
E-MAIL ADDRESS: **SamPull@gmail.com**		
ATTORNEY FOR (name): **Ima Dunn Hatchet**		

SUPERIOR COURT OF CALIFORNIA, COUNTY OF **Riverside**
STREET ADDRESS: **880 N. State Street**
MAILING ADDRESS:
CITY AND ZIP CODE: **Hemet 92543**
BRANCH NAME: **Hemet Courthouse**

PETITIONER: **Ima Dunn Hatchet**
RESPONDENT: **Barry D. Hatchet**

DECLARATION FOR DEFAULT OR UNCONTESTED ☑ DISSOLUTION ☐ LEGAL SEPARATION	CASE NUMBER: **XYZ123456**

(NOTE: Items 1 through 12 apply to both dissolution and legal separation proceedings.)

1. I declare that if I appeared in court and were sworn, I would testify to the truth of the facts in this declaration.

2. I agree that my case will be proven by this declaration and that I will not appear before the court unless I am ordered by the court to do so.

3. All the information in the ☐ amended ☑ Petition ☐ Response is true and correct.

4. Type of case (check a, b, or c):
   a. ☐ **Default without agreement**
      (1) No response has been filed and there is no written agreement or stipulated judgment between the parties;
      (2) The default of the respondent was entered or is being requested, and I am not seeking any relief not requested in the petition; and
      (3) The following statement is true (check one):
        (A) ☐ There are no assets or debts to be disposed of by the court.
        (B) ☐ The community and quasi-community assets and debts are listed on the completed current *Property Declaration* (form FL-160), which includes an estimate of the value of the assets and debts that I propose to be distributed to each party. The division in the proposed *Judgment* (form FL-180) is a fair and equal division of the property and debts, or if there is a negative estate, the debts are assigned fairly and equitably.
   b. ☑ **Default with agreement**
      (1) No response has been filed and the parties have agreed that the matter may proceed as a default matter without notice; and
      (2) The parties have entered into a written agreement regarding their property and their marriage or domestic partnership rights, including support, the original of which is being or has been submitted to the court. I request that the court approve the agreement.
   c. ☐ **Uncontested**
      (1) Both parties have appeared in the case; and
      (2) The parties have entered into a written agreement regarding their property and their marriage or domestic partnership rights, including support, the original of which is being or has been submitted to the court. I request that the court approve the agreement.

5. Declaration of disclosure (check a, b, c, or d):
   a. ☐ Both the parties have filed, or are filing concurrently, a *Declaration Regarding Service of Declaration of Disclosure* (form FL-141) and an *Income and Expense Declaration* (form FL-150).
   b. ☐ This matter is proceeding by default. I am the petitioner in this action and have filed a proof of service of the preliminary *Declaration of Disclosure* (form FL-140) with the court. I hereby waive receipt of the final *Declaration of Disclosure* (form FL-140) from the respondent.
   c. ☐ This matter is proceeding by default. I am the petitioner in this action, and service of the summons on respondent was done by publication or posting under court order. Service of the preliminary *Declaration of Disclosure* (form FL-140) is not required. I hereby waive receipt of the final *Declaration of Disclosure* (form FL-140) from the respondent.

Page 1 of 3

Form Approved for Mandatory Use
Judicial Council of California
FL-170 [Rev. January 17, 2020]

DECLARATION FOR DEFAULT OR UNCONTESTED
DISSOLUTION OR LEGAL SEPARATION
(Family Law)

Family Code, § 2336
www.courts.ca.gov

FL-170

PETITIONER: Ima Dunn Hatchet RESPONDENT: Barry D. Hatchet	CASE NUMBER: XYZ123456

d. ✓ This matter is proceeding as an uncontested action. Service of the final *Declaration of Disclosure* (form FL-140) is mutually waived by both parties. A waiver provision executed by both parties under penalty of perjury is contained on the *Stipulation and Waiver of Final Declaration of Disclosure* (form FL-144), in the settlement agreement or proposed judgment, or in another, separate stipulation.

6. ✓ Child custody and visitation (parenting time) should be ordered as set forth in the proposed *Judgment* (form FL-180).
   a. ☐ The information in *Declaration Under Uniform Child Custody Jurisdiction and Enforcement Act* (UCCJEA) (form FL-105)
      ☐ has ✓ has not changed since it was last filed with the court. *(if changed, attach updated form.)*
   b. ☐ There is an existing court order for custody/parenting time in another case in *(county):*
      The case number is *(specify):*
   c. ✓ The current custody and visitation (parenting time) previously ordered in this case, or the current schedule is *(specify):*
      As set forth in the Marital Settlement Agreement attached to Judgement (FL-180)

      ☐ Contained on Attachment 6c.
   d. ☐ The facts that support the requested judgment are *(In a default case, state your reasons below):*

      ☐ Contained on Attachment 6d.

7. ✓ Child support should be ordered as set forth in the proposed *Judgment* (form FL-180).
   a. If there are minor children, check and complete item (1) if applicable and item (2) or (3):
      (1) ☐ Child support is being enforced in another case in *(county):*
         The case number is *(specify):*
      (2) ✓ The information in the child support calculation attached to the proposed judgment is correct based on my personal knowledge.
      (3) ✓ I request that this order be based on the ✓ Petitioner's ✓ Respondent's earning ability. The facts in support of my estimate of earning ability are *(specify):*
         As set forth in the Marital Settlement Agreement attached to Judgement (FL-180)

         ☐ Contained on Attachment 7a(3).
   b. Complete items (1) and (2) regarding public assistance.
      (1) I ☐ am receiving ☐ am not receiving ☐ intend to apply for public assistance for the child or children listed in the proposed order.
      (2) To the best of my knowledge, the other party ☐ is ☐ is not receiving public assistance.
         ☐ Petitioner ☐ Respondent is presently receiving public assistance, and all support should be made payable to the local child support agency at the address set forth in the proposed judgment. A representative of the local child support agency has signed the proposed judgment.

8. Spousal, Partner, and Family Support *(If a support order or attorney fees are requested, submit a completed Income and Expense Declaration (form FL-150) unless a current form is on file. Include your best estimate of the other party's income. Check at least one of the following.)*
   a. ✓ I knowingly give up forever any right to receive spousal or partner support.
   b. ☐ I ask the court to reserve jurisdiction to award spousal or partner support in the future to:
      ☐ Petitioner ☐ Respondent
   c. ✓ I ask the court to terminate forever spousal or partner support for: ☐ Petitioner ✓ Respondent
   d. ✓ Spousal support or domestic partner support should be ordered as set forth in the proposed *Judgment* (form FL-180) based on the factors described in:
      ☐ *Spousal or Partner Support Declaration Attachment* (form FL-157)
      ✓ written agreement
      ☐ attached declaration *(Attachment 8d)*
   e. ☐ Family support should be ordered as set forth in the proposed *Judgment* (form FL-180).
   f. ☐ Other *(specify):*

**DECLARATION FOR DEFAULT OR UNCONTESTED
DISSOLUTION OR LEGAL SEPARATION**
(Family Law)

FL-170

PETITIONER: Ima Dunn Hatchet RESPONDENT: Barry D. Hatchet	CASE NUMBER: XYZ123456

9. [ ] **Parentage** of the children of the petitioner and respondent born prior to their marriage or domestic partnership should be ordered as set forth in the proposed *Judgment* (form FL-180).
   a. [ ] A voluntary declaration of parentage or paternity is attached.
   b. [ ] Parentage was previously established by the court in *(county):*
      The case number is *(specify):*
   [ ] The written agreement of the parties regarding parentage is attached here (Attachment 9b) or to the proposed *Judgment* (form FL-180).

10. [✔] **Attorney fees** should be ordered as set forth in the proposed *Judgment* (form FL-180).
   [ ] The facts in support of this request are on *Request for Attorney's Fees and Costs Attachment* (form FL-319).
   [✔] Other *(specify facts below):*
   As set forth in the Marital Settlement Agreement attached to Judgement (FL-180)

11. [ ] The judgment should be entered nunc pro tunc for the following reasons *(specify):*

12. [✔] Petitioner [ ] Respondent requests restoration of the former name as set forth in the proposed *Judgment* (form FL-180). *(proceedings for dissolution or nullity of marriage only)*

13. Irreconcilable differences have led to the irremediable breakdown of the marriage or domestic partnership, and there is no possibility of saving the marriage or domestic partnership through counseling or other means.

14. This declaration may be reviewed by a commissioner sitting as a temporary judge, who may determine whether to grant this request or require my appearance under Family Code section 2336.

STATEMENTS IN THIS BOX APPLY ONLY TO DISSOLUTIONS

15. If this is a dissolution of a marriage or domestic partnership created in another state, the petitioner or the respondent has been a resident of this county for at least three months and of the state of California for at least six months continuously and immediately preceding the date of the filing of the petition for dissolution of marriage or domestic partnership.

16. I ask that the court grant the request for a judgment of dissolution of marriage or domestic partnership based on irreconcilable differences and that the court make the orders set forth in the proposed *Judgment* (form FL-180) submitted with this declaration.

17. [ ] **Status only judgment:** This declaration is only for the termination of marital or domestic partner status. I ask the court to reserve jurisdiction over all other issues not requested in this declaration for later determination.

THIS STATEMENT APPLIES ONLY TO LEGAL SEPARATIONS

18. I ask that the court grant the request of a judgment for legal separation based on irreconcilable differences and that the court make the orders set forth in the proposed *Judgment* (form FL-180) submitted with this declaration.

I understand that a judgment of legal separation does not terminate a marriage or domestic partnership, and that I am still married or a partner in a domestic partnership.

---

19. [ ] Other *(specify):*

I declare under penalty of perjury under the laws of the State of California that the foregoing is true and correct.

Date: 03/20/2021

Ima Dunn Hatchet

Ima Dunn Hatchet
    (TYPE OR PRINT NAME)   (SIGNATURE OF DECLARANT)

**DECLARATION FOR DEFAULT OR UNCONTESTED
DISSOLUTION OR LEGAL SEPARATION**
(Family Law)

FL-180

ATTORNEY OR PARTY WITHOUT ATTORNEY *(Name, State Bar number, and address):*	FOR COURT USE ONLY
Ima Dunn Hatchet In Pro Per 1234 Rocky Road Splitsville CA 92395 TELEPHONE NO.: **951-555-1212** FAX NO. *(Optional):* E-MAIL ADDRESS *(Optional):* **SamPull@gmail.com** ATTORNEY FOR *(Name):* Ima Dunn Hatchet	

SUPERIOR COURT OF CALIFORNIA, COUNTY OF Riverside
STREET ADDRESS: 880 N. State Street
MAILING ADDRESS:
CITY AND ZIP CODE: Hemet 92543
BRANCH NAME: Hemet Courthouse

MARRIAGE OR PARTNERSHIP OF
PETITIONER: Ima Dunn Hatchet

RESPONDENT: Barry D. Hatchet

JUDGMENT	CASE NUMBER:

[✓] **DISSOLUTION** [ ] **LEGAL SEPARATION** [ ] **NULLITY**
  [ ] Status only
  [ ] Reserving jurisdiction over termination of marital or domestic
     partnership status
  [ ] Judgment on reserved issues
Date marital or domestic partnership status ends:
	XYZ123456

1. [ ] This judgment [ ] contains personal conduct restraining orders [ ] modifies existing restraining orders.
    The restraining orders are contained on page(s) _____ of the attachment. They expire on *(date):*

2. This proceeding was heard as follows: [✓] Default or uncontested [ ] By declaration under Family Code section 2336
    [ ] Contested [ ] Agreement in court
    a. Date: Dept.:   Room:
    b. Judicial officer *(name):*   [ ] Temporary judge
    c. [ ] Petitioner present in court   [ ] Attorney present in court *(name):*
    d. [ ] Respondent present in court   [ ] Attorney present in court *(name):*
    e. [ ] Claimant present in court *(name):*   [ ] Attorney present in court *(name):*
    f. [ ] Other *(specify name):*

3. The court acquired jurisdiction of the respondent on *(date):* 02/13/2021
    a. [✓] The respondent was served with process.
    b. [ ] The respondent appeared.

THE COURT ORDERS, GOOD CAUSE APPEARING

4. a. [✓] Judgment of dissolution is entered. Marital or domestic partnership status is terminated and the parties are restored to the
        status of single persons
        (1) [✓] on *(specify date):*
        (2) [ ] on a date to be determined on noticed motion of either party or on stipulation.
    b. [ ] Judgment of legal separation is entered.
    c. [ ] Judgment of nullity is entered. The parties are declared to be single persons on the ground of *(specify):*

    d. [ ] This judgment will be entered nunc pro tunc as of *(date):*
    e. [ ] Judgment on reserved issues.
    f. The [✓] petitioner's [ ] respondent's former name is restored to *(specify):* Dunn
    g. [ ] Jurisdiction is reserved over all other issues, and all present orders remain in effect except as provided below.
    h. [✓] This judgment contains provisions for child support or family support. Each party must complete and file with the court a
        Child Support Case Registry Form (form FL-191) within 10 days of the date of this judgment. The parents must notify the
        court of any change in the information submitted within 10 days of the change, by filing an updated form. The *Notice
        of Rights and Responsibilities—Health-Care Costs and Reimbursement Procedures and Information Sheet on Changing a
        Child Support Order* (form FL-192) is attached.

Form Adopted for Mandatory Use Judicial Council of California FL-180 [Rev. July 1, 2012]	**JUDGMENT** **(Family Law)**	Family Code, §§ 2024, 2340, 2343, 2346 www.courts.ca.gov

Page 1 of 2

FL-180

CASE NAME (Last name, first name of each party):	CASE NUMBER:
— In Re Marriage of Dunn; Ima and Barry	XYZ 123456

4. i. ☑ The children of this marriage or domestic partnership are:

(1) ☑ Name   Birthdate
       Kay Oss Hatchet   03/212017
       Upton O'Good Hatchet   09/19/2014

(2) ☐ Parentage is established for children of this relationship born prior to the marriage or domestic partnership

j. ☑ Child custody and visitation (parenting time) are ordered as set forth in the attached

     (1) ☑ Settlement agreement, stipulation for judgment, or other written agreement which contains the information required by Family Code section 3048(a).
     (2) ☐ *Child Custody and Visitation Order Attachment* (form FL-341).
     (3) ☐ *Stipulation and Order for Custody and/or Visitation of Children* (form FL-355).
     (4) ☐ Previously established in another case. Case number: Court:

k. ☑ Child support is ordered as set forth in the attached

     (1) ☑ Settlement agreement, stipulation for judgment, or other written agreement which contains the declarations required by Family Code section 4065(a).
     (2) ☐ *Child Support Information and Order Attachment* (form FL-342).
     (3) ☐ *Stipulation to Establish or Modify Child Support and Order* (form FL-350).
     (4) ☐ Previously established in another case. Case number: Court:

l. ☑ Spousal, domestic partner, or family support is ordered:

     (1) ☐ Reserved for future determination as relates to ☐ petitioner ☐ respondent
     (2) ☑ Jurisdiction terminated to order spousal or partner support to ☑ petitioner ☑ respondent
     (3) ☐ As set forth in the attached *Spousal, Partner, or Family Support Order Attachment* (form FL-343).
     (4) ☑ As set forth in the attached settlement agreement, stipulation for judgment, or other written agreement.
     (5) ☐ Other *(specify):*

m. ☑ Property division is ordered as set forth in the attached

     (1) ☑ Settlement agreement, stipulation for judgment, or other written agreement.
     (2) ☐ *Property Order Attachment to Judgment* (form FL-345).
     (3) ☐ Other *(specify):*

n. ☑ Attorney fees and costs are ordered as set forth in the attached

     (1) ☑ Settlement agreement, stipulation for judgment, or other written agreement.
     (2) ☐ *Attorney Fees and Costs Order* (form FL-346).
     (3) ☐ Other *(specify):*

o. ☐ Other *(specify):*

Each attachment to this judgment is incorporated into this judgment, and the parties are ordered to comply with each attachment's provisions. Jurisdiction is reserved to make other orders necessary to carry out this judgment.

Date:

5. Number of pages attached: _____

                                 JUDICIAL OFFICER
                           ☐ SIGNATURE FOLLOWS LAST ATTACHMENT

NOTICE

Dissolution or legal separation may automatically cancel the rights of a spouse or domestic partner under the other spouse's or domestic partner's will, trust, retirement plan, power of attorney, pay-on-death bank account, transfer-on-death vehicle registration, survivorship rights to any property owned in joint tenancy, and any other similar property interest. It does not automatically cancel the rights of a spouse or domestic partner as beneficiary of the other spouse's or domestic partner's life insurance policy. You should review these matters, as well as any credit cards, other credit accounts, insurance policies, retirement plans, and credit reports, to determine whether they should be changed or whether you should take any other actions.

A debt or obligation may be assigned to one party as part of the dissolution of property and debts, but if that party does not pay the debt or obligation, the creditor may be able to collect from the other party.

An earnings assignment may be issued without additional proof if child, family, partner, or spousal support is ordered.

Any party required to pay support must pay interest on overdue amounts at the "legal rate," which is currently 10 percent.

       JUDGMENT
                     (Family Law)

In Regard to The Marriage of Ima Dunn Hatchet AND Barry D. Hatchet
Case No.: XYZ123456

MARITAL SETTLEMENT AGREEMENT
AND
STIPULATION FOR JUDGMENT THEREON

THIS MARTIAL SETTLEMENT AGREEMENT and STIPULATION FOR JUDGEMENT, is made and entered into by and between Ima Dunn Hatchet, hereinafter referred to as Petitioner, AND Barry D. Hatchet, hereinafter referred to as Respondent.

WITNESSETH:

WHEREAS, the parties hereto are now married, and certain marital differences now exist and have existed for some time between them and said parties are now and for some time past have been living separate and apart; and,

WHEREAS, it is the intention of both parties hereto that their relation with respect to property and financial matter and maintenance and support be settled and finally established in this agreement in such a manner that any action respecting the rights or obligations of either toward the other that may now exist or hereafter arise, shall be conclusively settled and determined or as otherwise stated by this agreement; and,

WHEREAS, the parties are desirous of entering into a settlement of their property rights, and any and all claims for spousal support and maintenance, and desire to segregate and divide all the property owned and claimed by each of them so that each may have their share free and apart from the control of the other; and,

WHEREAS, the parties were married on October 10, 2000 and ever since the date of their marriage were living together as spouses until the date of their separation on January 22, 2021; and there are two (2) minor children of this marriage, to wit:

1. Kay Oss Hatchet, Date of Birth, 12/23/2017, age 3, daughter

2. Upton O'Goode Hatchet, Date of Birth 03/02/2014, age 6, son

1

CHILD CUSTODY

1. **Jurisdiction.** This Court has jurisdiction to make child custody orders in this case under the Uniform Child Custody Jurisdiction and Enforcement Act (Fam. Code §§ 3400-3465).

2. **Notice and opportunity to be heard.** The responding party was given notice and an opportunity to be heard, as provided by the laws of the State of California.

3. **Country of habitual residence.** The country of habitual residence of the child or children in this case is the United States.

4. **Penalties for violating this order.** If you violate this order, you may be subject to civil or criminal penalties, or both.

5. **Child Custody.** The parties have given considerable thought to the question of their child(ren)'s custody and in what manner the best interest of their child(ren) may be served. The parties concluded that custody of the minor children of the parties is awarded as follows:

Child's Name	Birth Date	Legal Custody to:	Physical Custody to:
Kay Oss Hatchet	12/23/2017	Joint	Joint
Upton O' Goode Hatchet	03/02/2014	Joint	Joint

6. In exercising joint physical custody of the child(ren), both parents shall share the physical care, custody and control of the child(ren) reasonably between them in such a manner as to insure that the child(ren) maintains frequent and continuing contact with both parents.

7. In exercising joint legal custody, the parents shall share in the responsibility and consult in good faith on matter concerning the health, education and welfare of the children.

8. Each parent shall notify the other of the name and address of each health practitioner who examines or treats the children; such notification to be made within 3 days of the commencement of the first such treatment or examination.

9. Each parent is authorized to take any and all actions necessary to protect the health and welfare of the children, including but not limited to consent to emergency surgical procedures or treatment administered to the child(ren).

10. Each parent will have access to the child(ren)'s school, medical and dental records and the right to consult with those professionals providing services to the child.

11. Each parent shall be designated as a person the children's school is to contact in the event of an emergency.

VISITATION

1. Visitation (Parenting Time) for **Respondent** shall be as follows:

    a. **Alternate Weekends** starting on February 5, 2021: from *Friday at 6:00 p.m.* through *Sunday at 6:00 p.m.*; and

    b. **Alternate Weekdays** starting on February 10, 2021: from Wednesday at 5:00 p.m. to Thursday at 5:00 p.m or as the parties may otherwise agree.

2. All time not specifically allocated to non-custodial parent shall be allocated to the custodial parent.

HOLIDAY SCHEDULE

Even	Odd	Holidays	Time
Petitioner	Respondent	July 4th	9:00a.m. until 7:00p.m.
Petitioner	Respondent	Halloween	9:00a.m. until 7:00p.m.
Respondent	Petitioner	Thanksgiving	9:00a.m. until 9:00p.m.
Petitioner	Respondent	Christmas Eve/Day	8:00 a.m. Christmas Eve thru 8:00 p.m. Christmas Dau
Yearly	****	Mother's Day	9:00a.m. until 7:00p.m.
****	Yearly	Fasether's Day	9:00a.m. until 7:00p.m.
Petitioner	Respondent	Kay Oss Hatchet Birthday March 21	9:00a.m. until 7:00p.m.
Petitioner	Responden	Upton O' Goode Hatchet Birthday 09/2014	9:00a.m. until 7:00p.m.

VACATIONS

1. Each parent may take a vacation of up to *two (2) weeks each year*. The vacationing parent must notify the other parent verbally or in writing of his/her vacation plans a minimum of *thirty (30)* days in advance, and, provide the other with a basic itinerary that includes dates of leaving and returning, destinations, flight information, and telephone numbers for emergency purposes.

2. The other parent has ten (10) days to respond if there is a problem with the schedule. Should the parent's dates conflict *Respondent* shall have preference for his/her dates in the ODD numbered years and *Petitioner* shall have preference for his/her dates in EVEN numbered years.

3

3.   Any vacation outside the United States requires prior written consent of the other parent or a court order.

CHILD SUPPORT

1.   *Repondent* shall pay to, for the support of the minor child(ren), the sum of ONE-THOUSAND FIVE HUNDRED TWENTY-ONE AND NO/100 ($1,521.00) per month, payable one half (1/2) on the first (1st) and one half (1/2) on the fifteenth (15th) days of each month *commencing March 1, 2021* and continuing until further order of court, or until the child marries, dies, is emancipated reaches age 19, or reaches age 18 and is not a full-time high school student, whichever occurs first.

2.   As and for additional child support for the minor child, the parents shall maintain the following listed life insurance policies naming the minor child as the irrevocable beneficiary of an amount not less than any current amount in place, until further order of court, or until the child marries, dies, is emancipated, reached age 19, or reaches age 18 and is not a full-time high school student residing with a parent, whichever occurs first.

3.   We agree that we are fully informed of our rights under the applicable guidelines for child support.

4.   We make this agreement freely without threat, coercion or duress and the needs of our child will be adequately met under this agreement.

5.   This agreement is in the best interest of our child(ren).

6.   The right to support has not been assigned to any county and no application for public assistance is pending.

SPOUSAL SUPPORT

1.   *Respondent* shall pay to *Petitioner* as and for spousal, the sum of $521.00 per month, payable one-half on the 1st and one-half on the 15th day of each month, commencing March 1, 2021 and continuing until the earliest of (1) the death of either party; (2) remarriage, or registration of a new domestic partnership of the party receiving support, (3) further order of the court.

4

DIVISION OF PROPERTY

     1.   The following property, whether community or separate, is awarded/confirmed to the Petitioner as the separate property of the Petitioner along with any and all encumbrances thereon and Petitioner shall timely pay, defend, indemnify and hold Respondent harmless therefrom:

         a. Petitioner's personal possessions and adornments:
         b. The miscellaneous household furniture, furnishings and equipment currently in Petitioner's possession;
         c. Wedding Ring
         d. 2020 Chevy Subrurban
         e. Acme Bank, Checking, acct. end. 1235
         f. Cash on Hand in the safe
         g. 350 Shares Pepsi Co.
         h. Ima's IRA
         i. One-half of Barry's 401(k)

     2.   The following property, whether community or separate, is awarded/confirmed to the Respondent as the separate property of the Respondent along with any and all encumbrances thereon and Respondent shall timely pay, defend, indemnify and hold Petitioner harmless therefrom:

         a. Respondent's personal possessions and adornments;
         b. The miscellaneous household furniture, furnishings and eqipment currently in Respondent's possession;
         c. Wedding Ring
         d. 2018 Subaru Forester
         e. Acme Bank, Savings, acct. end. 5678
         f. 2020 Income Tax Refund
         g. 200 Shares Exxon/Mobile
         h. One-half of Barry's 401(k)

DIVISION OF DEBTS

     1.   The following debts are awarded/confirmed to the Petitioner as Petitioner's separate debts and Petitioner shall timely pay, defend, indemnify and hold Respondent harmless therefrom:

         a. Any and all debts in the name of the Petitioner except as may be specifically herein stated to the contrary.
         b. Any and all debts incurred by Petitioner subsequent to the date of separation of the parties.
         c. Visa Credit Card

     1.   The following debts, whether community or separate, are awarded/confirmed to the Respondent as Respondent's separate debts and Respondent shall timely pay, defend, indemnify and hold Petitioner harmless therefrom:

a. Any and all debts in the name of the Respondent except as may be specifically herein stated to the contrary.
b. Any and all debts incurred by Respondent subsequent to the date of separation of the parties.
c. Master Credit Card
d. American Express Credit Card

2.   Petitioner and Respondent shall hold the other free and harmless from, and fully indemnify the other, for any debt, liability or other obligation incurred in connection with property received by each party individually pursuant to this agreement. Each of the parties will be liable to indemnify the other for any professional fees incurred by a party to defend against any action brought against that party in connection with property received by the other party individually under this Agreement, regardless of whether the action is unfounded or not and in connection with any debt to be paid by the other party pursuant to this agreement.

DISPOSITION OF REAL PROPERTY

1.   The parties hereto had acquired during the term of the marriage real property located at 1234 Rocky Road in the city of Splitsville, County of Nowhere State of California 92395.

2.   It is agreed by and between the parties hereto that said real property will be sold and the parties hereto agree the net equity therefrom will be divided equally. Prior to the sale of said property, both parties equally shall pay for the cost of the mortgage(s) and for the cost of maintenance and property taxes until such time as said real property is sold.

EQUITY EQUALIZATION

1.   The parties acknowledge that the above division does not constitute and equal division of property; however both knowingly, freely and without duress or undo pressure waive and release all rights and claims to receive an equalizing payment from the other party at any time.

RETIREMENT OR PENSON PLANS

In consideration of the agreement herein and in consideration of all the circumstances surrounding this agreement, Petitioner hereby assigns to Respondent, and Respondent hereby assigns to Petitioner, any and all of their respective right, title and interest to any Pension or Retirement Plan of the other party now existing or which will accrue at any future date with their respective employers.

WAIVERS

Each party waives any claim of credit and/or reimbursement he or she may have of the other party other than as may be specifically herein set forth. Each party specifically waives all right to reimbursement for the following:

6

(a) Epstein credits (In re Marriage of Epstein (1979) 24 Cal. 3d 76, 154, Cal Rptr. 413) and all rights to reimbursement to which a party may be entitled as a result of the payment of community obligation since the date of separation;

(b) (In re Marriage of Watts (1985) 171 Cal. App. 3rd 366, 217 Cal. Rptr. 301) and all rights to reimbursement to which a party or the community may be entitled as a result of one party's use of community assets since separation;

(c) All rights to reimbursement under Family Code §2640 or otherwise for separate property contributed to the acquisition or maintenance of community property.

(d) All rights to reimbursement under Family Code §2641 or otherwise due to community for contributions made by the community or either of the parties to the education or training of a party; and

(e) Jeffries Credits (In re Marriage of Jeffries (1991) 228 Cal. App. 3d 548, 278 Cal. Rptr. 830) and all rights to reimbursement to which a party or the community may be entitled as a result of one party's use of community assets since separation or one party's payment of debts and/or mortgage payments.

TAX DEFICIENCIES

1. The parties having filed joint federal and state income tax returns for most calendar years for which they were eligible. It is agreed that if for any jointly filed year federal or state income tax liabilities are claimed against the parties, they will:

2. If and only if the error which gave rise to the claim was actually known to both parties at the time the tax return(s) were filed, the parties shall be equally responsible for the claim, should same be actually imposed; on the other hand,

3. If the claim is based upon an error not so known, the parties shall first determine the amount of tax each would have been required to pay as married filing separately (not single). In determining that tax, the item causing the income tax liability will be allocated to, and included in the separate return of, the spouse who would have been responsible had the parties each filed separate income tax returns for the year(s) in dispute. Each party will pay only that portion of the tax liability claimed to be due as is caused by an increase in that spouse's income or by disal¬low¬ance of that spouse's deductions which would have been due if separate returns had been filed.

ATTORNEY FEES AND COSTS

Each party will bear all of his or her own attorney fees and costs incurred in connection with the negotiation, preparation, and execution of this agreement and proceeding dissolution.

DISCOVERY RIGHTS

1. Petitioner and Respondent each acknowledges that he/she has been advised, prior to the execution of this agreement of the availability of further informal and formal discovery procedures, accounting procedures, appraisals and investigative efforts as to the nature, extent and value of assets and obligations of the parties and other matters pertaining to the marital

dissolution of the parties. The parties further represent and acknowledge that each has entered in this stipulated judgement without relying on further discovery as authorized by law, in order to obtain early, amicable and expeditious settlement of the dissolution of the parties' marriage.

2.   Petitioner and Respondent each acknowledge that the parties have acquired various real and personal properties of unknown or speculative values. It is understood by the parties that neither party has made or is now making any representations, promises or warranties to the other regarding the value of any properties which are or may be community by nature. Each party has conducted his or her own discovery and investigation regarding property values and has consulted with professionals as deemed necessary. Each party relies upon his or her own discovery, investigation, assessment and judgement concerning the value of all properties. Therefore, each party waives and relieves the other party from the fiduciary obligation of disclosure of material facts and information regarding values required by Family Code §§1100 and 2105.

GENERAL PROVISIONS

1.   Both parties acknowledge that each of them has read this agreement, that each party understands and is satisfied with its' provisions and its' legal effect, that each party requests that its' provisions becoming binding when executed by both parties.

2.   The orders set forth herein shall be effective immediately upon the parties and their attorneys executing this agreement.

3.   In the event there is reconciliation of the parties after the date of execution of this agreement, this agreement and each of its' provisions shall nevertheless continue in full force and effect until it is modified or abrogated by another written instrument to that effect signed by each of the parties.

4.   This agreement, except as otherwise expressly provided herein, shall be binding on, and shall insure to the benefit of the respective parties, their heirs, executors, administrators, assigns, and successors in interest.

5.   In the event any provision of this agreement is held by a Court of competent jurisdiction to be invalid, void, or unenforceable, the remaining provisions shall nevertheless continue in full force and effect without being impaired or invalidated in any way.

6.   The parties are aware of Family Code §2024 advising parties to a dissolution of marriage to review their wills, insurance policies, retirement benefit plans, credit cards, credit accounts, credit reports, and other matters that they may wish to change. The parties are advised to review all property rights and employment benefits that have survivorship or inheritance factors (including, without limitation, life insurance, pensions, trusts, jointly held real and personal property, and bank accounts) to ensure that each expresses the present intent to the parties, particularly with respect to title and beneficiary designation.

8

NOTICE AND OPPORTUNITY TO BE HEARD

The responding party was given notice and an opportunity to be heard as provided by the laws of the State of California.

PENALTIES FOR VIOLATING THIS ORDER

Petitioner and Respondent each acknowledge being informed that in the event of violation of any provision contained in this agreement, the violating party may be subject to civil or criminal penalties, or both.

ENTIRE AGREEMENT

This Marital Settlement Agreement and Stipulation for Judgment contains the entire agreement of the parties on these matters, superseding any previous agreement between them.

MODIFICATION BY SUBSEQUENT AGREEMENT

The provisions of this agreement may be modified by subsequent agreement of the parties only by an instrument in writing signed by both of them, an oral agreement to the extent that the parties execute it, or an in-court oral agreement made into an order by a Court or competent jurisdiction.

MISCELLANEOUS

1.   Except as otherwise provided in this agreement, each party hereto does hereby waive any and all right to inherit the estate of the other at his or her death, or to take property from the other by devise or bequest (unless under a Will executed subsequent to the effective date hereof), or to claim any family allowance or probate homestead, or to act as administrator or administratrix of the estate of the other (except as the nominee of another person legally entitled to such right), or to act as executor or executrix under the Will of the other (unless under a Will executed subsequent to the effective date hereof).

2.   Petitioner and Respondent each acknowledge that the values of the assets awarded to each party pursuant to this agreement are subject to varying opinions. Each party further acknowledges that he or she had made such independent investigations with respect to such values (or waived the right to do so) so as to satisfy himself or herself that the economic terms and conditions of this settlement are fair and reasonable. Each party further recognizes that one or more of the said assets may be sold or otherwise disposed of for a value higher or lower than presently believed by such party. Each party waives and releases any claims that he or she might have in the event that any such assets are, in fact, hereafter sold or otherwise disposed of for a value more or less than, or different from, the value presently believed by such party. Each of the parties acknowledge that any or all claims for credits and/or reimbursements that either of the parties may have is resolved and settled by the terms of this agreement.

3.   Petitioner and Respondent each acknowledge that the division of property and allocation of debt as herein provided may not in actuality be an equal division of property and allocation of debt subject to the equalization sum as herein ordered; but each of the parties acknowledge that the division of property and allocation of debt as herein provided for is the agreement of the parties freely and voluntarily entered into without threat or duress, and that each of the parties deems the division of property and allocation of debt as herein set forth to be equal, subject to the equalization sum as herein ordered.

4.   Petitioner and Respondent hereto stipulate and agree that each has made a full and complete disclosure of all of his or her properties and that neither has knowledge of any property of any kind or nature in which the party so agreeing has any beneficial interest, except that property identified, listed, and distributed herein. If it is later discovered that either party has possession or control of, or has disposed of by gift or conveyance, an undisclosed beneficial interest in any community property, such party, on demand, shall transfer and assign to the other party one-half (1/2) of the interest therein or shall pay to the other party a sum equal to one-half (1/2) of the fair market value of such beneficial interest.

5.   The Court reserves jurisdiction to implement and enforce the executory provisions of this Judgment.

6.   Each of the parties shall, on demand, make, execute, and deliver any and all instruments or conveyances of any kind or character, furnish any information, or perform any other act reasonably necessary or proper to vest any property rights or estate exclusively in the other or otherwise to effectuate perform, or carry out the terms and provisions of this judgment without undue delay or expense. Either party who fails to comply with this paragraph and the provisions of the Judgment shall reimburse the other for any expenses, including attorney fees and court costs, that as a result of this failure become reasonably necessary for carrying out this judgment.

7.   Except for any debts or obligations of either party to the other created under this Judgment, each party shall pay and hold the other harmless from all personal debts and obligations incurred by him or her since their separation, and if any claim, action, or proceedings is hereafter brought seeking to hold the other party liable on account of such debts and obligations, such party will, at his or her sole expense, defend the other party against any such claim, action, or proceeding.

8.   Neither party shall charge or cause or permit to be charged to or against the other, any purchase or purchases which either of them may hereafter make, and shall not hereafter create any engagements or obligations in the name of or against the other, and shall never hereafter secure or attempt to secure, any credit upon or in connection with the other, in his or her name, and each of them will promptly pay all debts and discharge all financial obligations which each may incur for himself or herself, and each of them will hereafter hold the other free and harmless from any and all debts and obligations which the other may incur.

9.   The Court shall retain jurisdiction to make further orders which are necessary to enforce the provisions of this judgment.

10

10.   The parties shall hereafter own and hold the property received by him or her, respectively, by the terms hereof, and likewise all salaries, earnings and other property hereafter acquired by each of them, respectively, as his or her sole and separate property, free from any claims of the other (except as specifically provided for herein), or of any creditor of the other by reason of the community property laws of the State of California, or by reason of any other law or fact.

11.   Petitioner and Respondent are ordered that, within ten (10) days of written demand of the other, each party will execute any and all documents and instruments that the other may deem necessary to carry out the terms and provisions of this Judgement. In the event that either party refuses or fails to execute the necessary documents after the ten (10) day written demand period, then either party may apply, ex parte, on a twenty-four (24) hour notice to the other party and request the County Clerk, and said County Clerk is hereby authorized, to execute any document on behalf of the non-executing party as though the signature thereon has the same legal force and effect as if the party had signed it himself or herself.

12.   The parties retain their respective Social Security benefits, including any derivative rights to which they might be entitled by virtue of their marriage to each other, as their separate property pursuant to Federal law.

13.   Except as otherwise specifically herein provided, all property transferred herein is transferred subject to all existing liens and encumbrances thereon. The transferee of such property shall indemnify and hold harmless the other party for any claim or liability that the other party may suffer or may be required to pay on account of such encumbrances or liens. Each party represents to the other that all such liens in their amounts are accurately and specifically referred to herein. Any liens not disclosed herein shall be deemed as missed and significant liability.

14.   Except as otherwise provided herein, whether or not third parties make claim against either or both parties, and whether or not formalities of title have been completed, each party shall, and does, release the other from any and all liability, whether primary, derivative or vicarious, whether in tort, or in contract, or by statute, and shall hold the other harmless from all claims of the other relative to any vehicle awarded to each party respectively regardless of the present form or title. Nothing herein shall provide for or be interpreted as reducing the insurance coverage.

15.   The Court reserves and retains jurisdiction to make further orders necessary or appropriate to implement the provisions of this judgment dividing such plans and benefits.

Signature of the Parties

We have read this entire Martial Settlement Agreement and Stipulation for Judgment. We understand it fully and request the Court to make our stipulation and agreement the Court's judgment. We understand that the willful failure to comply with the provisions of this agreement may be a contempt of Court and may be punishable by fine and/or imprisonment.

11

We waive all further notice of this judgment.

Each of the parties declares and agrees that he or she has read this agreement and fully understands the same and each of the parties agree that the execution of this agreement shall be and is intended to be a full, complete, and final adjustment of all property rights of the parties existing as of the date hereof and supersedes any prior agreement between the parties written or oral. Each of the parties further agrees that this agreement is made and entered into by him or her of his or her own volition and with full knowledge of its legal effect. By signing in execution hereof each party agrees that this agreement is made at this or her individual request and after full and thoughtful consideration

Dated: 03/20/2021

Ima Dunn Hatchet

Ima Dunn Hatchet

State of California
County of Riverside

On March 21, 2021, before me, Jodi Silbermann, Notary Public,   personally appeared

Ima Dunn Hatchet

who proved to me on the basis of satisfactory evidence to be the person(s) whose name(s) is/are subscribed to the within instrument and acknowledged to me that he/she/they executed the same in his/her/their authorized capacity(ies), and that by his/her/their signature(s) on the instrument the person(s), or the entity upon behalf of which the person(s) acted, executed the instrument.

I certify under PENALTY OF PERJURY under the laws of State of California that the foregoing paragraph is true and correct.

WITNESS my hand and official seal.

SIGNATURE_____

PLACE NOTARY SEAL ABOVE

12

Dated:

Barry D. Hatchet
_____
Barry D. Hatchet

State of California
County of Riverside

On March 21, 2021, before me, Jodi Silbermann , Notary Public,

personally appeared Barry D Hatchet_____

who proved to me on the basis of satisfactory evidence to be the person(s) whose name(s) is/are subscribed to the within instrument and acknowledged to me that he/she/they executed the same in his/her/their authorized capacity(ies), and that by his/her/their signature(s) on the instrument the person(s), or the entity upon behalf of which the person(s) acted, executed the instrument.

I certify under PENALTY OF PERJURY under the laws of State of California that the foregoing paragraph is true and correct.

WITNESS my hand and official seal.

SIGNATURE_____

PLACE NOTARY SEAL ABOVE

IT IS SO ORDERED.

Dated:

_____
JUDGE/COMMISSIONER OF THE
SUPERIOR COURT

13

ACKNOWLEDGMENTS

To my tribe: my daughter, mom, grandma, sister, and nephew, your love and support means everything to me and helped me become the success I am today.

My daughter, Ashley, you are my ride 'r die for life. Near or far, you are the wind beneath my wings!!

Mom, Laury Silbermann, thank you for always loving us unconditionally and always being there for us.

My sister, Amy Silbermann, you are my rock and know me better than anyone. Thank you for always being there.

Ashley Evenson and Noah Arrue, you are each proof of resilience through adversity. I am beyond proud of the strong, smart and determined individuals you have each become.

Dr. Sidney Weissman, my grandfather, taught me to be strong, adventurous, and independent.

Eleanor Weissman, my grandmother, there are no words to express my love for you. My love for travel comes from you. You are always my biggest champion. I love you big time!

My dad, Barry D. Silbermann, I am happy we are all back in each other's lives. My legal path started with going to the office on weekends with you.

Ginger Hitzke, I am both honored and grateful to call you my friend. Thank you for our weekly accountability meetings, along with the endless support and encouragement you have shown during this process. You are an inspiration and a genuinely kind, smart, and empowering woman. You truly are an angel.

Dr. Alicia Wilkins, you are such an inspiration to me. I am forever grateful for that day you knocked on my door, during your campaign. It led me to your beautiful space at *Hera Hub*, which facilitated making my dreams into reality and finally finding that *place* where I belong. I am honored and grateful to be a part of the *Hera Hub* and to call you my friend.

In loving memory of Merrill Schulze, your sweet, kind and loving spirit will live on in our memories. Fly with the angels Lady in Red!

Carnell Johnson, Jr. "...Ocean views, small circle, it's the chosen few, I wrote it down and I followed through..." ~ Nipsey Hussle ~

THANK YOU FOR READING MY BOOK!

DOWNLOAD YOUR FREE GIFTS

Read This First

Just to say thanks for buying and reading my book, I would like to give you a few free bonus gifts, no strings attached!

To Download Now, Visit

www.Divorce101.org/FreeGifts

I appreciate your interest in my book, and I value your feedback as it helps me improve future versions of this book. I would appreciate it if you could leave your invaluable review on Amazon.com with your feedback. Thank you!

REFERENCES

Cal. Family Law Code Sections Code §§1-20100 et. Seq. (Deerings 2020)

Superior Court of The State of California, Judicial Council

https://www.courts.ca.gov/policyadmin-jc.htm,

accessed May 25, 2021

"Fear: False Evidence Appearing Real." — Unknown 73 Inspirational Quotes on Fear

By Henrik Edberg Updated January 11, 2021

https://www.positivityblog.com/22-inspirational-

quotes-on-fear

2017 Court Statistics Report — Judicial Council of California

Project Eve Reinvent your career;

https://projecteve.com/10-great-quotes-women- change/

Lack of clarity is the primary reason for failure in business and personal life. Brian Tracy, Peter Chee, 12 Disciplines of Leadership Excellence Https://www.wow4u.com/clarity quotes.html

— Dolores Huertahttps://sasforwomen.com/divorce-quotes-inspirational/

Psychology Today- Five Types of High-Conflict Personalities And their targets of blame—and sometimes violence; Bill, LCSW, JD, Psychology Today. Retrieved from:

https://www.psychologytoday.com/us/blog/5-types-people-who-can-ruin-your-life/201711/five-types-high-conflict- personalities#

Psychology Today – Gaslighting. Psychology Today. Retrieved from

https://www.psychologytoday.com/us/basics/gaslighting

The Wittiest Quotes on Divorce. Psychology Today. Retrieved from:

https://www.psychologytoday.com/us/blog/evolution-the-self/201211/the-wittiest-quotes- divorce.

Who Initiates Divorce More Often? Are women or men more likely to initiate divorce? Psychology Today.

Marston, William Moulton, 1893-1947. Wonder Woman. New York: Holt, Rinehart and Winston, 1972.

National Statistics Domestic Violence Fact Sheet https://www.ncadv.org/statistics

https://www.usatoday.com/story/money/2020/01/21/divorce-how-much-it-costs-to-get-divorced-in-every-state/41010675/ The cost of divorce: How much do you pay to get divorced in California vs. Colorado?

Hristina Byrnes, The cost of divorce: How much do you pay to get divorced in California vs. Colorado. Byrens, Hristina, 24/7 Wall Street

HARVARD.pdf Description of California Courts' Programs for Self- Represented Litigants –prepared for meeting of the International Legal Aid Group –Harvard, June, 2003By Bonnie Rose Hough

https://www.aamft.org/About_AAMFT/About_Marria

ge_and_Family_Therapists.a spx

https://www.greatlakesdfs.com/blog/life-after-divorce-quotes"When we deny our stories, They define us. When we own our stories, we get to write the ending." – Brené Brown edition LMFT

170 Inspirational Quotes for Women on Strength and Leadership. Retrieved from:

https://everydaypower.com/inspirational-quotes-for-women/

Lisa Kleypas, Blue-Eyed Devil. Retrieved from: https://lisakleypas.com/blue-eyed-devil

Poem: "The Voice," by Shel Silverstein

70 Inspirational Divorce Quotes to Help Move On.
Weiner, J. (n.d.). retrieved from:
https://everydaypower.com/divorce-quotes/
accessed: May 25, 2021

Made in the USA
Las Vegas, NV
29 June 2021